Queen
Victoria

Elizabeth Longford

Sutton

Series Editor C.S. Nicholls

Highly readable brief lives of those who have played a
significant part in history, and whose contributions still
influence contemporary culture.

———————————————————

First published in 1999 by
Sutton Publishing Limited · Phoenix Mill
Thrupp · Stroud · Gloucestershire · GL5 2BU

This edition published in 2005

ISBN 0 7509 4049 2

Typeset in 11.5/15pt Perpetua.
Typesetting and origination by
Sutton Publishing Limited.
Printed and bound in England by
J.H. Haynes & Co. Ltd, Sparkford.

CONTENTS

For Frank

A C K N O W L E D G E M E N T S

I would like to thank Lady de Bellaigne and all her staff at the Royal Archives for permission to use the Letters and Journals of Queen Victoria, and other material in the Archives. I am particularly grateful for permission to publish for the first time the letter written by Queen Victoria to her doctor Sir Charles Locock, on the controversial subject of her daughters nursing their babies. I must also thank my agent Mike Shaw, my friend John Murray, my daughter Antonia Fraser and my granddaughter Flora Soros.

CHRONOLOGY

1819	**24 May**. Alexandrina Victoria born, Kensington Palace.
1820	**23 January**. Victoria's father, Edward Augustus, fourth son of George III, dies.
	29 January. George III dies. George IV ascends the throne.
1830	George IV dies. William IV ascends throne.
1837	**24 May**. Victoria's eighteenth birthday.
1837	**20 June**. William IV dies. Victoria ascends throne at eighteen.
1838	**28 June**. Victoria crowned, Westminster Abbey.
1839	**15 October**. Victoria proposes to Albert.
1840	**10 February**. Marries Albert, Chapel Royal.
1840	Victoria, Princess Royal born.
1841	Albert, Prince of Wales born.
1843	Alice born.
1844	Alfred born.
1846	Helena born.
1848	Louise born.
	Year of Revolutions, King Louis-Phillipe of France escapes to England.
1850	Arthur born.
1851	Crystal Palace built, Great Exhibition opened.
1853	Leopold born.
1854–6	Crimean War.
1855	**April**. State visit by French Imperial couple, Napoleon III and Eugénie.
1857	Beatrice born.
	Albert given title of Prince Consort.
1858	Princess Royal marries Prince of Prussia.
1861	**14 December**. Albert dies.
1861–9	Victoria's seclusion.

Chronology

1863	Prince of Wales marries Denmark's Princess Alexandra. Baron Stockmar dies.
1864	Prussia, under Bismarck, invades the Duchies.
1865	Lord Palmerston dies. Victoria's uncle Leopold, King of Belgians, dies. John Brown brought south on advice of Dr Jenner to entice the Queen into fresh air.
1868	**January**. Disraeli becomes Prime Minister.
1868	**November**. Disraeli defeated by Gladstone. *Leaves from the Journal of our life in the Highlands 1848–61* published.
1869	Victoria fifty years old.
1870	Franco-Prussian War, Napoleon III defeated and forced to abdicate. 'Royalty Question' arises in England and there are calls for Victoria's abdication.
1872	**27 February**. Victoria emerges for first official public appearance to attend thanksgiving service held at St Paul's for her heir's recovery from typhoid.
1874	**February**. Disraeli in power again.
1876	**May Day**. Queen Victoria declared Queen-Empress of India, Britain and Ireland.
1881	**April**. Disraeli dies.
1883	**29 March**. John Brown dies.
1887	**20 June**. Golden Jubilee Day.
1891	**13 March**. Prince of Wales's eldest son dies, leaving George V next in line to the throne.
1897	**20 June**. Diamond Jubilee Day: sixty years of rule by Queen Victoria.
1898	Gladstone dies. Boer War begins.
1901	**22 January**. Victoria dies.

BORN TO BE QUEEN, 1819–37

Q ueen Victoria gave her name to a great era. Only the subjects of Elizabeth I and Victoria are known by the name of their Queen. Was Queen Victoria herself great? The presumption is yes. Certainly, with her 9 children, 41 grandchildren and 87 great-grandchildren, her fertility would seem greater than that of English women now alive. They called her the Grandmother of Europe.

Yet she did not quite grow to 5 feet tall nor did she outgrow her childhood's sloping chin. And she gave Europe, through her daughters' marriages, not only the blood royal but also the scourge of haemophilia, carried unknown to all with her own genes. Nor was her conception so much immaculate as competitive, geared to win the 1818 royal marathon race for the throne. Any saintliness that Victorians sometimes saw in their Queen's rotund, ageing image, was never traced from her father the Duke of Kent, who married her mother only months after dismissing Madame de St Laurent, his faithful mistress for nearly twenty-eight years.

It was the death in childbirth in 1817 of Princess Charlotte, heir to the throne, that made Princess Victoria important. Her father, Edward Augustus, fourth son of George III, had made his career in the army. A successful campaigner in the West Indies, he might have reached the top but for his unpopularity due to excessive discipline, culminating in the execution of three mutineers at Gibraltar. He was retired to England, where he lived chiefly on credit until 1815, when he withdrew to Brussels to economise. Princess Charlotte and her husband Prince Leopold of Saxe-Coburg urged him to solve his problems by marrying Leopold's widowed sister, Princess Victoria of Leiningen. After Charlotte's untimely death Edward did so. The handsome pair – he tall with dyed brown hair and whiskers and blue eyes, she with brown eyes and black ringlets – were married at Kew Palace on 11 July 1818. The German-speaking Duchess had her speeches written out for her in phonetic English: '. . . ei em môhst grêtful for yur congratuleschens end gud uishes. . . .' Nine months later an unwieldy caravanserai consisting of German maids, a female German doctor-midwife, cage-birds and lap-dogs hurried the heavily pregnant Duchess from the Continent to Calais – driven by the Duke himself to save money – so that England's heir might be born on English soil. The Duchess had promised the Duke a son. But it was Alexandrina Victoria who arrived at Kensington Palace in the spring dawn of 24 May 1819.

The family's first months together were cheerful enough. The Duke was a doting father. Intensely proud of his infant daughter, he would hold her up to his friends for their inspection, bidding them look well for one day she would be Queen of England. His friends included Whigs and even radicals like Sir Matthew Wood, populist mayor of London who was to champion the unruly Queen Caroline against George IV; and Robert Owen the socialist of New Lanarkshire Mills.

But when Christmas 1819 was over, so too was the Kents' family life. There was nothing whatever wrong with the baby, for she had been nursed by the practical Duchess, already the experienced mother of two children by her first husband. The Duke was immensely amused and curious about this operation, for most aristocrats hired wet nurses. Unfortunately, when it came to his own health, the Duke took the wrong advice. His boyhood tutor, Dr John Fisher, now Bishop of Salisbury, recommended Devon as a cheap, healthy resort. On the way there the Duke caught a chill in the icy Salisbury Cathedral, and found the winds of Sidmouth whipped it to fever-pitch. He was persuaded to make his will by John Conroy, his equerry, and was visited by Dr Stockmar, valued German secretary-physician of his brother-in-law Prince Leopold.

On 23 January 1820 the Princess Victoria lost her father to what had become virulent pneumonia. He was followed to the grave six days later by his father George III, the Prince Regent becoming George IV. As Victoria's uncle, he had shown bad-tempered jealousy at her christening, having refused to allow the tiny intruder to be called Georgiana after him or Charlotte after his dead daughter. She could be called after her mother. So she was christened Alexandrina after the Tsar of Russia and Victoria after her mother; but the grand 'Alexandrina' was shortened, and she became the humble 'Drina' for the first years of her life.

The new King could at least have paid for the royal exiles to return from Sidmouth but that labour of love was left to Uncle Leopold who brought them back to Kensington Palace. Admittedly Parliament had endowed Prince Leopold with £50,000 a year on marrying Charlotte. Victoria was almost certainly the heir, for what stood in her way? 'Uncle King', as she called George IV, would have no more legitimate children after Charlotte, and his successor William IV, another marathon runner like Edward, produced only four legitimate children, who all died. Immediately after Victoria in the line of succession came the Duke of Cumberland who was also King of Hanover, but this villainous-looking 'wicked uncle' was unthinkable as England's king. So Victoria it must be. Before she became Queen, however, there were plenty of opportunities for her royal uncles to influence her, if not to finance her.

What had she inherited from her father? Nothing in the way of wealth. Only debts. And this would be one of the difficulties her mother had to cope with in her upbringing. (One of Queen Victoria's very first acts on ascending the throne was to pay off Papa's debts.) Mentally and emotionally she owed much to Edward. There was his strong sense of duty and discipline, often unpopular, but balanced by humanitarian instincts: he abolished flogging in his unit and founded the first regimental school. Victoria was to show both traits – the strictness and the sympathy – though she disliked schooling, regimental or otherwise, and adored the ballet. He was artistic and loved his sketchbook. So did she. His exaggerated sense of military discipline was balanced by an admirable personal sense of duty, which she and her descendants shared. At heart he was a true Hanoverian: so was she – until she married Albert.

During her first years Drina did not speak and hardly heard a word of English. All around her were musical German voices, notably those of her mother, her half-sister Princess Feodore and Fraülein Lehzen, Feodore's governess. Lehzen's services were passed on to Drina after Feodore got married in 1828 and left for the Continent. Princess Victoria was three before she began to learn English as a second language. It is often asked whether Queen Victoria had a German accent: the answer is no. She had a very good ear as part of her musical endowment. However, there was a certain precision about her speech that told the true story of her early linguistic experience.

What of her destiny? Her household apparently believed that she passed her childhood in total ignorance. However, even if the German attendants never breathed a word, it is hard to credit her English nurse, Mrs Brock, with such inhuman restraint. Nor did Sir Walter Scott, for example, reject the legend that a little bird had whispered to Victoria the truth. Contemporary anecdotes suggest that she must have known something. Says Princess Victoria to her little friend while playing at Kensington: 'You must not touch those; they are mine; and I may call you Jane, but you must not call me Victoria.'[1] At least she knew she was different.

Another day, while visiting Royal Lodge, Windsor, with Mama, her 'Uncle King' dashed up in his phaeton, ordered them to 'Pop her in' and was off again. It was exhilarating. She did not flinch from the rouged royal cheek, and laughed at Mama's fear of her falling out. In reality the Duchess was terrified lest the King, put up to it by Cumberland, should kidnap the child heir. Why did the Duchess fall for the rumour of a Cumberland Plot to supersede Victoria? She was fed it by her ambitious majordomo, Sir John Conroy, who had a plot of his own. Under the delusion that his wife, Lady Conroy, shared the blood royal, Sir John treated the Duchess and Princess with familiarity, regarding himself as semi-royal. His secret plan was to become Victoria's private secretary the moment she ascended the throne. To this end he would have to isolate Kensington completely from Windsor.

His spectacular power-plan was to have three separate results. First, Victoria always felt that her childhood was sad and lonely, cut off as she was from her natural associates in the royal family. Second, the Duchess's reputation was unjustly and permanently besmirched by Conroy's familiarities. Many influential people such as the Duke of Wellington and Charles Greville the diarist interpreted Conroy's behaviour as the possessiveness of a lover. Third, an unbridgeable abyss opened in Kensington Palace between the two factions: on one side the Duchess supported by and supporting Conroy, Charles Leiningen (Victoria's half-brother) and the spinster Princess Sophie, another Palace inhabitant; on the anti-Conroy side, Princess Victoria herself, supported solely but slavishly by Baroness Lehzen.

By the time George IV had died (1830) and William IV was on the throne, Conroy had worked out a scheme for dealing with the ever more recalcitrant Victoria. The ailing William IV would die, Conroy hoped, before Victoria was eighteen (her majority), whereupon her mother would rule as regent with Conroy at her elbow. However, two incidents had already showed the stuff of which Victoria was made.

On 11 March 1830, at the age of eleven, she was 'accidentally' shown by Lehzen during a history lesson her exact place in the succession — much nearer than she thought. After a storm of tears she gave her hand as if in solemn pledge and pronounced the famous words, 'I will be good.' (Queen Victoria was later to confirm that she had indeed spoken thus.[2]) Five-and-a-half years later, in October 1835, she was lying at Ramsgate sick with typhoid, having collapsed after one of those strenuous country-wide tours organised by Conroy to show her to the people. Conroy decided this was the psychological moment to force the sixteen-year-old invalid to sign a statement that he, Conroy, should be private secretary when she became Queen. After she was indeed Queen, she told Lord Melbourne her first Prime Minister how she fought Conroy off: 'I resisted in spite of my illness.' 'What a blessing!' smiled the Prime Minister.[3]

The run-up to her accession was unendurable. Her birthday on 24 May 1837, when she attained her majority, brought no joy, though her poor old uncle gave her a piano and tried to give her money, which Mama made her refuse. As the miserable days passed she saw nobody but Lehzen. Conroy had subjugated all Kensington but these two. Even Prince Charles Leiningen believed that Victoria must somehow be made to sign away her freedom to Conroy: '*she must be coerced*', he said.[4] But Conroy knew in his heart that the Duchess would never have the courage to lock up her daughter, as he and Charles wished.

And so on the early morning of 20 June 1837 Victoria was descending the awkward little staircase at Kensington Palace, having slept in her mother's bedroom for the last time. Her Uncle William had died at twelve minutes past two, and she was Queen at eighteen years and twenty-seven days. For a glorious year her heart bubbled up in spontaneous happiness. Above all it was wonderful always getting her own way. When Mama and Lord Melbourne insisted, for propriety's sake, on her attending a review at Hyde Park in a carriage rather than on horseback, she refused. The amused ballad-makers put her point of view in verse:

> I will have a Horse, I'm determined on that,
> If there is to be a review.
> No horse, no review, my Lord Melbourne, that's flat,
> In spite of Mama and of you.

She loved her work, even the endless communications from her ministers, and having her hands kissed nearly 3,000 times at a levée. Moneywise, she kept intact her sense of economy instilled over the years by Lehzen, putting aside the whole of her first Privy Purse to paying off Papa's debts. Her Civil List was an unbelievable £385,000. It was indeed her *annus mirabilis*. The diarist Thomas

Creevey saw her at Brighton Pavilion, laughing so loud that she showed her not very pretty gums.

Crowned in Westminster Abbey on 28 June 1838, she ran straight upstairs immediately afterwards to give Dash, her spaniel, his bath.

The man whose looks and words by now haunted her imagination was Lord Melbourne, whom she wrote about so much in her journal that he quickly became 'Lord M'. Lonely and hitherto rather cynical, he took a unique pleasure in offering a new, sophisticated vision of life to the young Queen. 'What happened to those poor Irish who were evicted by their landlords?' she once asked. (The Whigs under Melbourne had recently applied coercion and martial law to suffering, rebellious Ireland.) 'They become *absorbed* somehow or other,' replied Lord M. – which made the Queen and Prime Minister laugh 'amazingly'.[5] The great Whig was not altogether a good influence, but she desperately needed love and self-confidence, and he gave her both.

After the coronation, Queen Victoria's relations with the Duchess deteriorated and so did her own peace of mind. She now called Lehzen her 'mother'. In revenge, the anti-Lehzen set spread hurtful rumours of 'foreign influences' at Court. One peculiarly damaging story concerned Mama suddenly entering Victoria's room to find her Uncle Leopold's secretary-doctor Stockmar sitting with her and all her state boxes open in front of him! The rift between mother and daughter ran through all the ladies of both households, but Melbourne stubbornly insisted that such rifts were common. He rejected all the Duchess's offers to dismiss Conroy – well provided for, of course. Victoria's personal actions were continually criticised by Mama: she had failed to give her mother due precedence at the coronation.

Why did not Uncle Leopold guide his niece and sister in this imbroglio? He was no longer Victoria's essential father-figure after Lord M. came along. Moreover, Leopold had married again and acquired a new family and a new job — King of the Belgians. His niece desperately needed a totally fresh guide, though she did not yet realise it. When Leopold sent Stockmar to be a liaison, it served only to step-up the hostile propaganda. Stockmar left in 1838.

Yet despite everything, Victoria had never lost her early popularity. Her 'Royal Progresses', as William IV sarcastically called her tours of England and Wales, had left her family rifts virtually unknown. Though wilful, she still seemed deliciously innocent, blushing at her first Privy Council. And it was an advantage to follow two 'wicked uncles' — Monarchs are so often judged by comparisons and contrasts. However, even with all her advantages, things could and did get worse.

It began as usual with 'Ma & J.C.', as Victoria now curtly referred in her journal to her mother's partnership with John Conroy. Victoria was already sad and indignant at the thought of Melbourne's future and the Whigs' inevitable defeat by the Tories, when it became apparent that Lady Flora Hastings, Mama's lady-in-waiting, was showing a swollen stomach. Lady Flora came from a great Tory family. Lehzen and Victoria, and probably also Melbourne, jumped to the conclusion that Lady Flora was '*with child*!!' by J.C. The Queen forbore to mention even in her journal the name of the 'Monster & demon Incarnate' whose mistress Lady Flora surely was, but his initials appeared, she said, as the first words of the second line of that page. The horrific initials were J.C.[6] The Queen was to assure the Prime Minister that neither she nor Lehzen had ever confided their suspicions to anyone. Nevertheless Queen

Victoria and her foreign baroness were responsible for the spreading of the scandal in the public mind.

During the next few months things were to get worse for the Queen both in Parliament and the Palace. The political disaster she dreaded above all – losing her Whig government – seemed to be at hand. On 22 March 1839 the Whig policy of reform of plantations in Jamaica was defeated in the House of Lords. The emotional Queen burst into tears at the thought of 'ALL ALL my happiness being at stake' and could hardly stop crying.[7] As she sat with Melbourne nearly a month later, 17 April, both of them lamenting the situation in Parliament and the Palace, a sudden thought came to her: at least there was an alternative to the latter, to life with Mama and that wretched Lady Flo. Marriage. Yes, she could marry Prince Albert of Saxe-Coburg, as Mama and Uncle Leopold wished. But it was a 'schocking [*sic*] alternative'. Suppose she married Albert and he took Mama's side? She dismissed the 'schocking' alternative from her mind.[8]

Three days after the 'schocking' alternative had presented itself, 'new horrors' connected with the Jamaica Bill loomed up. Sure enough on 7 May Melbourne came to her with news of his resignation, together with two pieces of thoroughly bad advice for her as Queen. First, she should send for the old Duke of Wellington and persuade him to become Tory leader, and so the new Prime Minister, in place of Sir Robert Peel, the actual party leader. Wellington, of course, declined. Melbourne's *bêtise* showed how far even professional politicians were from understanding the way the party system would develop. No wonder Queen Victoria was to make mistakes.

Melbourne's second bad suggestion caused Victoria's first big political mistake. Known to history as the Bedchamber Crisis, it sprang from Victoria's refusal on 9 May to permit Peel to exchange any of her household ladies for Tories – not even those married to active Whigs. No doubt Melbourne had put her up to it; no doubt she herself mistakenly believed that Peel's wish to change *some* of her ladies was merely an undercover way of ousting Lehzen. Nevertheless, as she taunted the nervous Peel, who shuffled from one foot to the other like a dancing-master, she showed a natural, spontaneous wit worthy of a better cause. In a life of Queen Victoria it is both relevant and delightful to remember her stinging question to poor Peel: Were the Tories so weak that they needed even the *ladies* to be of their opinion? And her gleeful account of the interview to Lord Melbourne, with its unwitting prediction of women's emancipation: 'I should like to know if they mean to give the Ladies seats in Parliament?'[9]

And so Peel withdrew, battered and deeply hurt. Melbourne was again the triumphant Queen's Prime Minister and for a short while she was again a pleasure-loving girl. She even gave a grand ball, officially in honour of a Russian Grand Duke, but really to celebrate the return of her happiness and the rescue of the knight in shining armour from the Tory dragon by the fair lady herself, and not vice versa. On the day of Melbourne's resignation she had lamented as before in her journal, 'All, ALL my happiness gone! That happy peaceful life destroyed . . .' Now that happiness, embodied by 'dearest, kind Lord Melbourne' as her Minister, was recaptured, restored and surely safe for years.

Not so. As Parliament improved, the Palace darkened. The Hastings family were using the press to defend Lady Flora's innocence and blacken her enemies. As the Queen drove up the course at Ascot she was jeered at as 'Mrs Melbourne!' Soon it was a rare pleasure *not* to be hissed at the opera. Melbourne's return had put Society and the Tories even more against her than before. Then came the tragic news that Lady Flora was dying.

What could the Queen do — no heartless girl as the public imagined — but visit her? After all, while Victoria was defiantly calling Lehzen her mother, Flora was thanking the Duchess for being a mother to her. On 27 June the dying woman received the Queen, whose journal carried a genuinely moving account of the farewell visit, emotional and without the usual capital letters. She noticed particularly 'the searching eyes, the grasp of the hand as if to say, "I shall never see you again" . . .'[10], which was no more than the truth, for she died eight days later on 5 July. Lady Flora had asked to be finally justified by a post-mortem. Her family agreed, provided it was not performed by Sir James Clark, the Court doctor. (He had failed to quash the first Palace rumours of the lady's pregnancy.) So an independent post-mortem revealed that she had died from a liver tumour. At dead of night her funeral cortège set out for Loudoun, joined by a mourning carriage sent by the Queen. Only one or two people threw stones at it — something that at this point had to be reckoned as good news.

It was high time to start turning over a great many new leaves, on one of which was already written the legend 'schocking alternative', or simply 'alternative'.

PRINCE ALBERT:
A SAFE HAVEN

Victoria's Uncle Leopold, King of the Belgians, was a man of great acumen. No doubt with the help of his clever secretary-doctor, Baron Stockmar, he reduced Victoria's psychology to a matter of simple staging – first stage, Lord Melbourne. She doted on him, and through him loved older people. Then, in September of the crucial year 1839, Uncle Leopold arranged for his niece to be visited by her cousins the Ferdinand Coburgs, Augustus and young Leopold, brothers of the King of Portugal. These jolly cousins gave her a compelling taste of youthful, warm Coburg family life. After they had left she could not bear to talk familiarly to the old. Come back Coburgs. Come Albert.

He arrived on the evening of 10 October and the small dignified Queen received him at the top of the stone staircase in the high Windsor quadrangle. He was with his elder brother Ernest who would one day inherit the dukedom of Saxe-Coburg and Gotha. Both were handsome, upstanding young men but they had had a horrible Channel crossing. Albert brought with him a load of queries: Uncle Leopold had warned Albert that Victoria had said she might like him only as a cousin, not as a husband – and even if she liked him as a husband, she could not face marriage for two or three years at the earliest, and . . . and . . .

But the first sight of Albert changed everything in a flash. He was beautiful. Cousin Alexander Mensdorff, who had come with the 'Ferdinands', was handsome, but Albert was *beautiful*. She wrote it in her journal that evening: 'It was with some emotion that I beheld Albert – who is *beautiful*.' She could not have put it clearer than that. But later she did fill in the 'broad shoulders', the 'fine waist' and 'slight but very slight' whiskers.[1] It was true that Albert had already visited Victoria when they were both seventeen but that had been a colourless companionship, sleepy, too, for he did not like staying up late. And there had been no lovely greyhound, Eos, to show Albert off. Eos, meaning Dawn, had been taught to walk around the luncheon table eating food delicately from forks. Victoria was in love with Albert not as a cousin but as a future husband, and on Tuesday 15 October she proposed to him (it had to be her act) and they fell into each other's arms.

* * *

Victoria and Albert, although first cousins, were complementary rather than similar. True, they possessed intense love of music in common. But an examination of their strikingly similar childhood utterance, both at aged eleven, might suggest that they were far more alike than in fact they were. As against Victoria's 'I will be good', Albert is reported as saying, 'I wish to be a good and useful man.' But the true meaning of the word 'good', as used by each, exposes the radical difference in their characters. Whereas solemn young Albert was speaking almost in the spirit of a knightly vow, Victoria was mainly concerned with promising dearest Lehzen to do her lessons better in future.

The differences between them when they were first married soon became manifest. Though both were dutiful and high minded, it was he who revelled in the solution of knotty problems, while she was working from a state of contentment and pleasure, if not frivolity, towards a deeper interest in real issues. She loved the town and he loved the country; but she was ready to learn and he to teach. She rarely felt unwell, he not infrequently. Each, however, had had an unhappy childhood and now needed love.

In a sense each had lost a father, Victoria's by death and Albert's by gross misbehaviour towards his mother (though Albert still somehow revered him), divorcing her for the same sin that he himself had committed obstinately and often. With their mothers feelings were equally intense but in reverse. Albert's beloved mother remarried and died young. Victoria's mother haunted every corner of the home but was reduced to a mere 'Ma' in the journal. Perhaps Victoria expected Albert to send 'Ma' away, as Albert's own mother had been banished. But the pieces on the board were not to behave as Victoria expected and the stumbling-block was not to be 'Ma', but the Queen's surrogate mother, dearest Lehzen.

The wedding was fixed for 10 February 1840 in the Chapel Royal. Victoria had designed her bridesmaids' white satin dresses decorated with wheat-sheaves, no doubt with the Hungry Forties in mind: Victoria had a good concrete imagination. But all was not plain-sailing for Albert. Those vile Tories were making a fuss about his allowance, his precedence over the old royal family and his religion. Was he one of those Catholic Coburgs? The Queen vented her rage in her journal. 'Monsters! You Tories shall be punished. Revenge, revenge!'[2] Nevertheless the little Queen was not yet ready to make sacrifices for Albert. His suggestions for an extended honeymoon at Windsor resulted in the Queen mounting her high horse. 'You forget, my dearest

Love', she wrote to him on 31 January, 'that I am the Sovereign, and that business can stop and wait for nothing.'[3] He was not likely to forget again. The honeymoon, at Windsor, was to last only two or three days. Nor was 'Ma' likely to forget the actual wedding. After the service was over the small figure in white, wearing a wreath of orange blossom, a diamond necklace and the sapphire brooch given to her by Albert, kissed her Aunt Adelaide but only shook the Duchess of Kent's hand.

As with all striking events, the wedding illustrated the contradictions in Victoria's character. The thing she most enjoyed about the service was not any assertion of sovereignty but the simplicity – the way in which the Queen of England and Prince Consort were just referred to by Christian name: ' "Victoria, wilt thou have, &c . . ." "Albert, wilt thou &c . . ." ' Moments of simplicity, however, were prolonged into a huge wedding breakfast, followed by a quick change into a gown trimmed with swansdown and a dash to Windsor – 'I & Albert alone, which was SO delightful.' But it was still not 'Albert & I', as Queen Elizabeth II would say 'My husband and I'; and it is probable that Albert felt more alone than his wife did. In any case it was an exhausting, racketty drive to Windsor, with well-wishers galloping on either side of them, and Victoria finally collapsed on her sofa with Albert sitting beside her on a footstool: '. . . I NEVER NEVER spent such an evening!!! . . . & his excessive love & affection gave me feelings of heavenly love & happiness, I never could *have hoped* to have felt before! – really how can I ever be thankful enough to have such a *husband*!'[4]

The first few weeks and months of marriage continued to be 'SO delightful', though they were not quite so delightful for Albert. He did not tell anybody at first. When the Queen endlessly signed her state papers, Albert would help with the blotting-paper – and perhaps would also pick up some crumbs of information from the table. The busy little Queen may indeed have thought of drawing Albert into affairs of state bit by bit; but if she did, there was someone at hand to stop her. Baroness Lehzen, whose room had been located next to the Queen's, advised Victoria to treat Albert exactly as she treated her, Lehzen, over business matters. He should *not* be admitted into any confidence. And whereas he had told his wife that there must never be any secrets between them, the jealous, pathetic Lehzen believed that there should be almost nothing but secrets.

In another, grimmer sense, Albert not only wielded the blotting-paper but *was* the blotting-paper. It was to be his duty to mop up any emotion in the Queen surplus to the effective performance of her own essential job. Thus, if she felt depressed he could cheer her up – but he must not ask which political problem had brought on her depression, whether the Irish, or the falling revenue, or the knitters of Paisley or lace-makers of Honiton.

One day in May 1840 Prince Albert wrote a sad letter to his friend Prince William of Lüwenstein. He was not the master but only the husband in the house. And of course he ought to have been master as well. Though Albert may not have known it, the Duchess of Bedford was spreading the gossip that he was not even an effective husband.

All this was quickly proved to be rubbish, for in the summer it leaked out that Queen Victoria was pregnant. Albert would have preferred a formal announcement, but that was not the English way at this time. What Victoria had been unable to do for him herself (part of her longed to have Albert as her lord and master) their children swiftly accomplished. For he was soon helping her not only to blot her state papers but also to sit down, when pregnant, to draw on her stockings – and to get up again!

Their popularity climbed, and all the more rapidly because of the first attempt on the Queen's life, when Edward Oxford, an undersized, disturbed youth of eighteen, fired at her in the Mall on 10 June 1840. There were to be altogether seven weak-minded assailants over the years, though the Queen always firmly believed that they were in fact responsible for their actions. She felt thankful after the law was changed so that they could be punished instead of being condemned to death for treason and then reprieved. Oxford's attempt affected the lives of Victoria and Albert in different but positive ways: Victoria believed that she had been divinely preserved for some great purpose; Albert was appointed Regent in case of her death from violence or childbirth – a first step to becoming Master in the House.

On 21 November 1840, three weeks early, Victoria the Princess Royal was born. First known as Pussy or Pusette, she became Vicky soon after the Prince of Wales arrived less than a year later on 9 November 1841. Beginning impersonally as 'the Boy', he was to bear his father's blessed name, Bertie. The Queen, no baby-worshipper, judged them aesthetically, sketch book in hand, finding their action too froglike for beauty and their little bald heads better under caps. The standards in the royal nursery matched their mother's low expectations, the lady in overall charge being Mrs Southey, sister-in-law of the poet laureate but no winner of nursery laurels, being a prize muddler. Only the wet nurse seemed to be in place; she came from Cowes.

Meanwhile politics had at last arranged themselves to Queen Victoria's satisfaction; at least Victoria *thought* that politics had arranged themselves. In fact the resourceful Albert had acted behind the scenes, without Victoria's knowledge, when he realised in May 1841 that a falling revenue meant a falling Whig government. Victoria's high-handed action during the Bedchamber Crisis of 1839 had artificially created for Melbourne an extra two-year span. But now another Bedchamber Crisis might mean a falling monarchy. Victoria, already two months into her second pregnancy, was in no state to bargain with Peel over ladies. Instead the good Albert fixed up a new Tory Mistress of the Robes with the new Tory leader; Victoria was grateful – and Albert took several steps nearer to being the Master in the House. Even Melbourne's political farewell included excellent advice to Peel: he should tell HM everything – but in very few words. And Albert was ready with a final piece of good advice for Melbourne: Lehzen must go, as Lehzen would not work with the Tories, and Melbourne must tell Victoria this. Melbourne agreed but said Albert must tell Victoria. Albert said no.

Apart from Lehzen, there was calm at Court, Melbourne being happy to hand over his treasure to Albert, and Victoria able to bear the loss of Lord M. because of the gain of Albert. As for Lehzen, her fate was nigh – in the nursery. Baby Pussy was far from flourishing. She persistently lost weight despite being put on asses' milk by Sir James Clark, the Queen's doctor, and was terrified of her new brother. On 16 January 1842 a violent quarrel broke out between the alarmed parents, conducted through angry notes, floods of tears and finally the intervention of Baron Stockmar on Albert's side. Albert blamed his child's desperate condition on the state of the nursery and especially Lehzen's meddling. Panic-stricken, he referred to her as 'the yellow lady', for poor Lehzen now added jaundice to the charms of her long neck, quivering nose and pocketful of caraway seeds. At length Victoria realised she must choose between Lehzen and Stockmar – or even Albert. The Baron and Baroness couldn't remain at Court together.

The same Queen Victoria who had recently changed governments with no fuss, at last brought herself to change the government of the nursery. Explaining pathetically to Stockmar that she only flew into rages when feeling unwell, she gladly accepted the brilliant Lady Lyttelton as the new head of the nursery establishment.

As for the final departure of the Baroness, in the end it was not unworthy of her long years of royal service, though not altogether creditable to her employers. First, Albert arranged for the Queen to visit Scotland while Lehzen stayed behind to be with the children. They were parted at last! Finally came the morning of 30 September 1842 when the Baroness slipped away, as instructed, without telling or saying goodbye to the emotional Queen. Laden with the possessions of twenty years and a generous pension, Lehzen sailed back to Germany to devote her money to her brother's children. She and the Queen met now and then abroad, Lehzen outliving Albert, and Victoria far outliving Lehzen.

Over Baroness Lehzen the Prince Consort had become somewhat obsessive, using her as Victoria's scapegoat. All Victoria's faults (tempers, frivolity) were Lehzen's, all her virtues (dutifulness, devotion) were her own. Once Lehzen had gone, Prince Albert wrote about Victoria to his brother Ernest as being 'the most perfect companion a man could wish for'.[5] And it was only after Wellington persuaded Conroy and Albert ordered Lehzen to exit for the Continent that Queen Victoria was able to enter her own safe haven.

The emotional safety of her haven could now perhaps be guaranteed. Indeed she took the trouble to correct an entry in an old journal in which she had written of her happiness with dear Lord M. In those days, she noted, she had not yet discovered the meaning of 'real happiness'.[6]

There were many physical dangers, however, crowding in upon royalty in the mid-nineteenth century. In the early morning of 3 December 1840, for example, a boy with a passion for the Palace was found curled up under the Queen's dressing-room sofa. This was his third visit and he heard Pussy cry before he was seized. Known as 'the Boy Jones', he did time before doing well at sea.

The Palace's discomforts were trying: a waste pipe dripped outside the royal bedroom and two different departments laid and lit the fires, while two more cleaned the inside and outside of the windows, so that both sides were never clean at once. Here was old mess and muddle crying out for Albert's new broom. But when he stopped a notorious perk (an official collected hundreds of unused candles every morning) he was denounced as a saver of candle-ends. Meals were often late, the Queen apologising.

And of course the attempts on her life continued, no less alarming for being a bit mad. Two more came in 1842, the inspiration of John Francis and John Bean. Number four attempt was to come in 1846, when an Irishman fancied the idea of frightening the English Queen by disguising a kettle spout as a pistol. When that did not work he shot at the Queen on Constitution Hill with his landlady's pistol – but no bullet. Princess Helena, aged three, who was present, summed up her mama's thoughts, 'Man . . . must be punished' and William Hamilton was transported for seven years.

The royal children were more and more with their parents, apart from on occasions that might attract shootings. They were an essential part of Victoria's safe haven. She would write her journal with Vicky on her lap, while Albert played the organ with one infant on each knee. The babies came in a joyful stream, with never an infant lost nor their mother struck by illness. Vicky and Bertie were followed by Alice (Fatima or Fat Alice) in 1843, Alfred (Affie) in 1844 and Helena (Lenchen) in 1846. The Prince Consort was a naturally good, energetic father, dragging the babies about their nursery floor in a big basket. Queen Victoria, eager to be a good parent also, found it more difficult. She had not enjoyed lessons particularly as a child but now felt there were two subjects she could teach her children: religion and history. She had to get her half-sister Princess Feodore's advice on how to hear her children's prayers at night — kneeling by the bedside or what? Lutheran piety replied from Germany she should just let them sit up in bed. In history, the Queen made no secret of her own preference for the Stuarts.

She had had all her babies so far without 'aetherial aid', as anaesthetics were affectionately called, since chloroform was not yet generally available. The Queen's mother wished her daughter would space her family a little more; and the Queen herself was to urge spacing upon her own daughters (not of course by means of today's family planning) but Victoria had not practised what she preached. Indeed, she would probably have had even more than her nine children if Albert had lived longer. And yet she always called child-bearing the shadow-side of marriage.

* * *

What Queen Victoria now called her happy home life was not due only to her own energies. Prince Albert's creativeness was developing apace and contributing or taking over in more and more fields. His wife had once lamented that she could not create him King Consort. Now the Master in the House was spilling out into the Houses of Parliament. Sir Robert Peel had appointed him chairman of the Arts Commission for Parliament's rebuilding. And since 1842 Prince Albert had attended Her Majesty's audiences.

When a disagreeable little man from the press got through the crowds at Windsor to the castle terrace and reported unfavourably on Albert's health, Victoria agreed on the need for more country air and privacy. Melbourne considered the people of Kent the worst in the country and Victoria found those of Sussex worse still – the royal children were mobbed on the Walmer Road and the Queen on Brighton Pier. By 1843 they were discussing with Peel the purchase of Osborne House on the Isle of Wight in Hampshire.

The Queen of England had travelled in her first train in 1842. ('Not so fast next time, Mr Conductor' was said to have been her husband's comment.) Peel believed in communications and she believed in Peel. With the Hungry Forties upon them, she hoped to visit famine-stricken Ireland, she rationed bread at Buckingham Palace, and she backed the government's increased 'Maynooth Grant' for Catholic religious education, denouncing those Protestants who objected as bigots. Bigotry was always one of her dirtiest words. She also preferred helping individuals to supporting causes, since causes always seemed to attract agitators – another dirty word. She liked to concentrate on those three unlucky lighthouse keepers or that performing dwarf.

Nevertheless Peel's party – the Tories – should follow their leader in his efforts to cure the Irish potato famine. His policy, Corn Law Reform, would enable cheap imported corn to start replacing their diseased staple diet. If the Tories betrayed Peel and he resigned, the Queen would surely weep as passionately at Peel's departure as she had wept at the prospect of his arrival in 1839. But the unexpected was to happen.

With the good old Duke of Wellington's cooperation, Peel got Corn Law Reform through the House of Lords, but was defeated in the Commons on a severe Irish Coercion Bill to deal with lawlessness. The Peel government fell – but for once Victoria did *not* fall about with misery. Albert had steeled her nerves. Albert had given her a sense of proportion, enabling her to remain calm and therefore contented. She wrote in her journal on 8 June 1846, 'Really, when one is so happy & blessed in one's home life as I am, Politics (provided my Country is safe) must take only a 2nd. place.'[7] But was her country safe?

The new Foreign Secretary, Lord Palmerston, had been a popular Whig in Victoria's youth. Since the 1830s he had set up various of Victoria's royal relatives on European thrones: Leopold (Belgium), Maria (Portugal), Isabella (Spain). In Victoria's eyes, Palmerston's only fault, so far, was to have married Melbourne's widowed sister, Lady Cowper. Queen Victoria never approved of widows remarrying. As for her new Prime Minister, Lord John Russell seemed a typically partisan little Whig. She definitely preferred the way Sir Robert Peel kept virtually all the power in his own hands, whereas Russell was always consulting colleagues.

The Year of Revolutions, 1848, opened for the Queen without a warning note. Her journal began with her happiness – if only time would stand still – and Albert's usual wish to the family of '*Prost neu jahr!*' But it was not to be a good New Year. The tocsin sounded in February and by the 23rd, King Louis-Philippe of France had abdicated. Palmerston allowed Queen Victoria to send a steamer to rescue him from France – with suitable warnings. The French royal family escaped to England.

While Victoria was organising the French family, risings were threatening in Austria, Hanover, Bavaria, Naples, Schleswig-Holstein, Leiningen and even little Coburg. Only Belgium and England stood firm – and of course Russia for very different reasons. As a reward, England was presented with another royal baby. Princess Louise, the Queen's sixth child and born as she was in Revolution Year, convinced her mother that she would be something special. And indeed she was, being artistic, exceptionally long-lived and the first to marry a commoner.

The Queen's confinement ended on 3 April; but at their first breakfast together Victoria and Albert heard that a giant Chartist march was due on the 10th! Albert arranged the departure next day of the weeping Queen for Osborne in the Isle of Wight. There were no more tears and the Queen wrote to her Uncle Leopold, 'Great events make me calm.'[8] It was a brave thought but not entirely accurate. Albert and no other had made her calm.

As soon as Victoria reached the peace and primroses of Osborne in April, her volatile mood changed. She began to long for the excitements of action. But young Feargus O'Connor, leader of the Chartists, saw things the other way round. Trembling at the prospect of their march on Parliament from Kennington Common, he fervently shook hands when the Commissioner of Police ushered him and the other leaders into three cabs that drove them harmlessly to the House of Commons, where their petition was left 'lying on the table'.

Victoria and Albert were to experience many alarms before the Year of Revolutions was out, the worst being a rumour at Whitsun that a gang of determined Chartists was making its way to Osborne. All the local labourers were called in from the fields and armed with pitchforks before it was discovered that the fearful revolutionaries were merely a jolly party of Oddfellows on a Whitsun outing. So who were the odd fellows now?

Nevertheless the Queen, with the French royal family forever in her sights, had taken to praying for her own children, in whatever positions fate might land them, high or low. In fact her whole family were to continue 'high' in spite of the perils of the nineteenth century. But the Queen felt she must be prepared. In any case she must preach against revolution to whoever presented themselves, such as Lord John Russell, her Whig Prime Minister. The Whigs could hardly be expected to denounce revolution in principle, since they had created the Glorious Revolution when Victoria's favourite Stuarts went under. All the same, there were points to be made. One day that summer (6 August 1848), she gave Russell a piece of her mind on revolutions and the duties of sovereigns and people: 'Obedience to the Sovereign is obedience to a higher Power, divinely instituted for the good of the *people*, not of the Sovereign, who has equal duties &/ obligations.'[9]

THREE

THE AGE OF
IMPROVEMENT, 1849–56

The whole Victorian Age might be called an age of improvement, so many advances were made, from urban sanitation to free state education; and the basic belief was in things getting better. But these years of the royal marriage seemed to reflect the Age of Improvement in a very special way. To begin with, there were so many physical and material improvements in their family life, some necessary and all desirable. Buckingham Palace needed expanding to accommodate a Victorian family, and Parliament voted £20,000 to build the south-facing extension looking over the Mall and including the famous balcony. Queen Victoria was to appear on the balcony for the first time at the central mid-century event – the Great Exhibition of 1851.

Another personal improvement for the Queen had taken place earlier – her first sea bathe in 1847. This delightful benefit to health could itself be improved upon, as the Queen recorded with amusement when she saw the Belgian women bathing at Ostend and drying their long hair in the sun with no caps, so many 'like penitents'.[1] The Queen's bathing depended entirely on another major development in the family's life – holidays at Osborne – though the actual sea dips began as a rather pathetic matter of a hut with frosted-glass windows, a platform with curtains and a very nice protective bathing-lady.

Osborne was rebuilt to Albert's own Italianate design and became even more necessary after the Windsor 'Slopes' were invaded by commercial intruders who stole and published extracts from the Queen's sketch-book. The ceilings at Osborne were delightfully low compared with those of her Palace and Castle, and there was even a convenient 'little room' leading out of her bedroom. In her sitting-room she and Albert had their desks side by side, next to the blazing beech-log fire. But even the new Osborne could be improved upon. It had two failings: the climate of the Isle of Wight was too mild and relaxing to suit Albert's health; and it was too accessible to strangers, as had been shown in the Year of Revolutions, 1848. What the royal family needed was something bracing and remote. They needed Balmoral.

Balmoral itself was subjected to the benign yet rigorous law of improvement. When Victoria and Albert first arrived they found kilts were not worn. Soon the two little princes, Bertie and Affie, were running about everywhere in kilts, and it was kilts for all. The Queen, who was in and out of her house and around the village just like anyone else, noticed the visiting Clerk of the Council, Charles Greville, with approval. Characteristically, the Queen improved herself with her favourite dancing lessons (Scottish) while the erudite Albert sought for his own improvement in an enormous Gaelic dictionary. The two gillies to be first acclaimed in Victoria's journal were Grant and Macdonald, with whom she felt supremely 'safe'. On 11 September 1849 there appeared for the first but by no means the last time the name of one John Brown. This early Victorian Balmoral stood for the safe, the inaccessible and the bracing. It was only after Prince Albert's death that later Victorian mores invaded even the Highlands and Balmoral became 'Balmorality'.

The shield of happiness was pierced for a moment when Sir Robert Peel died on 3 July 1850, after a fall from his horse. 'Thy will be done', wrote the Queen in her journal, but the very next words were to adopt a tone of indignant protest that was to become all too familiar after another great man died in the next decade: 'but it does seem mysterious', she continued in 1850, 'that in these troubled times an essential leader like Peel should be removed.'[2]

The year after Peel's death, the Prince reached his zenith, creating at the same time the splendid peak of Victorian England's achievement. His wife may be said to have reached her zenith as a mother with the birth of her seventh child, Prince Arthur, on 1 May 1850. The old Duke of Wellington shared his birthday and became his godfather. He was Victoria's favourite son.

All Albert's creativeness came together in 1851 at the Great Exhibition of Work in a peaceable and friendly world. Instead of guns there was agricultural machinery and the swords had been beaten into American Bowie knives. Albert had found the men to spark it off: Joseph Paxton of the Chatsworth conservatories, who built a Crystal Palace over the elm trees in Hyde Park; Samuel Smiles who recommended 'Self-Help' to the workers. The exhibition was Albert's answer to the Chartists – and they still needed one. Six million visitors were to pay their entrance fees, the Queen visiting almost daily for three months. The Prussian royal family arrived and while Prince Frederick William escorted ten-year-old Victoria and her younger brothers and sisters round the stalls, the two mothers, Queen Victoria and Princess Augusta of Prussia, cosily plotted their children's nuptials.

Everything tiresome was successfully dealt with: the 'fashionables' of Society, who objected to the invasion of Hyde

Park, were disappointed in having no thunderstorms to break the glass. Wellington told the Queen how to drive out the sparrows that had flocked under the domes: 'Try sparrow-hawks, Ma'am.' When the Protestant Lord John Russell complained of too many Catholic crucifixes on view, Albert retorted that they were balanced by the number of pagan idols. And God seemed to have been forgiven for removing poor Peel: the motto of the Exhibition was, 'The earth is the Lord's and all that therein is.'

Though Victoria noticed how 'fagged' her brilliant Consort often was, she ended by abasing herself and her sex in a passion of hero-worship. 'We women are not *made* for governing.'[3]

The lofty, peaceful ideals of the Great Exhibition seemed at first to have borne fruit in British politics. Queen Victoria happily noted the satisfactory situation in the Foreign Office, where Lord Palmerston, the bellicose Whig Foreign Secretary, had proved too fond of 'gun-boat diplomacy' and after a fiasco with the so-called Don Pacifico case, when Palmerston tried to attach magic to British citizenship ('*Civis Romanus sum*') followed by his undiplomatic welcome of Napoleon III, he, Palmerston, was forced at last to resign. The Queen rejoiced in his successor, the gentlemanly Lord Granville, known as 'Pussy' – Palmerston was never a pussy – who obligingly kept Her Majesty informed on all issues, 'which Lord Palmerston had long ceased to do'.[4] However, the Whigs fell over a dispute about the militia within two months of Palmerston's own fall. The old villain called it his tit-for-tat.

The new Tory government of Lord Derby brought a fresh face and a fresh concept before Victoria. A minister named Benjamin Disraeli riveted her attention because of his oddity; this was not quite a passport to her approval but certainly not a disadvantage.

The fresh concept was Albert's and was imparted to Lord Derby: the Tories must help the Court to become a symbol for morality, despite Lord Melbourne's view that 'damned morality' would 'ruin us all'. As if to show how right Albert was, a miser named John Camden Nield died, leaving the moral Queen £250,000. The Queen herself believed she had been chosen because she would not waste it. The great Victorian identification of morality and saving was on the way.

* * *

In 1853 while peace still reigned, Queen Victoria made what might be called her greatest ever contribution to her people's happiness, particularly the women. When her eighth child, Prince Leopold, was born on 7 April, he was delivered with the help of chloroform. The Queen found it delightful, though there is no evidence that if the baby had been a girl she would have called it 'Anaesthesia', as one grateful mother did. Her subjects had followed the experiment closely, one indignant section of religious opinion arguing that a child produced without adequate pain would not be sufficiently loved. And when baby Leo later failed to thrive, emerging as the first haemophiliac in the family, there must have been voices to repeat that Mother Eve and her story should not be mocked. Nevertheless, Victoria and Albert, with their enthusiastic belief in improvement, were not to be deflected by controversy from the public good. When the Queen's last child arrived four years later there had been no renunciation of the wonder-drug and Princess Beatrice could indeed have been called Anaesthesia.

It was only after the Great Exhibition and the year 1851 that Victoria realised the force of Albert's energies and new ideas. The outbreak of the Crimean War in 1854 was to show her conclusively that the Prince would never lead a more restful life by her persuading others not to overload him with work. He would always be his own most relentless taskmaster.

The royal couple faced the war in totally different ways. Victoria revelled in an atavistic feeling that she was somehow leading the tribe to victory, and there was nothing she liked more than getting up really early to see a regiment march off. Welcoming any physical contact between herself and her soldiers, she loved the handshakes and appreciated their occasional refusals to have their medals engraved in case they did not get back the one their Queen had handed to them. (One of her favourite exhibits in 1851 had been a machine for making thousands of medals a minute.) She had no difficulty in believing that Nicholas I, the Tsar of Russia, was the enemy and that he intended to spread his empire all over Asia, with special danger to Britain's Empire in India. For had not the Tsar a personal weakness that explained all his bad behaviour? Victoria was a devoted adherent of her doctor Sir James Clark's fresh-air theories, and she had heard that the Russian family spent six months of every year with every window tightly sealed and not a breath of fresh air to keep them sane and sound.

For Prince Albert the first months of the war were bad ones. His enemies in society spread rumours of his being on the Russian side and a few broadsheets accusing him of treachery soon had the crowds converging on the Tower of London to watch Albert vanishing through the Traitors' Gate. Even the army, for which he worked so hard designing modern uniforms and helmets, resented the interference of this foreigner and when he suggested a German Foreign Legion to be raised for service with the British Army, they commented sarcastically, 'Why German? Why not Red Indian?'

Trouble arose for Victoria with public criticism of the War Cabinet in 1855. Albert could not help her in January when the notably unbellicose Lord Aberdeen resigned as Prime Minister and there was a concerted public demand for the return of Lord Palmerston. Known half affectionately, half ironically as the 'Whiskered Wonder', the 71-year-old Palmerston was by now deaf, blind and equipped with false teeth that his colleagues said would fall out if he tried to orate. The Queen, recognising her duty to find the country a government, drove frantically to and fro, trying possible combinations. Palmerston could be leader of the House of Commons, but who should be Prime Minister? Derby? Lansdowne? Russell? No. No. No. It had to be 'Pam' himself.

It is now possible to assess the effect of the Crimean War on the Queen as ruler. First, she asserted herself as the person responsible for the country's government and the army's strength. She also re-stated the historic belief in the semi-mystical connection between the army and the Monarchy, and through her, between the army and aristocracy. Her arguments about the army also applied to the Foreign Office, though less viscerally, so to speak. But despite the Queen's strong and increasing bonding with her military forces, the net result of the Crimean War was the army's reform. Its loyalty to Queen and Country was no longer found to depend on the mediation of the aristocracy, devoted as Lord Raglan and Lord Lucan were in their own way, but on a third party called Merit. The army's health and efficiency depended most definitely on professional and middle-class brains cultivated in a place named Sandhurst.

It is obvious that Prince Albert's part in the war, especially *vis-à-vis* Queen Victoria, would have been very different had he accepted the old Duke of Wellington's offer of the succession to his own exalted position as Commander-in-Chief. Yet Albert was right to refuse it. The job would and ought to be all-demanding, and Albert already had his work cut out in serving the Queen and their family. As for Lord Palmerston, the Queen was to find that when supported by a sensible Foreign Secretary like Lord Clarendon, old 'Pam' was the best Prime Minister she and Albert had had.

A couple who added greatly to the nervous excitement of the Queen's war were the Emperor and Empress of the French, Napoleon III and his tall, elegant, auburn-haired wife Eugénie. France was Britain's ally against the Tsar of Russia, and Napoleon had served as a special constable while in exile in London during the Chartist rising. As such, it was doubly appropriate that the glamorous French Imperial pair should pay a state visit to Victoria and Albert at Windsor during April 1855. The Tsar had died shortly before, in March, it was said from heartbreak after the horror stories of Inkerman. To have a Napoleon dining in the Waterloo Chamber was history. The Empress Eugénie brought with her the first crinoline. That was history too.

The Queen finally sat in on a council of war at Windsor, one of the great experiences of her life. It made her feel right inside everything at last. There was only one awkward moment when the Emperor proposed to go out himself to Sebastopol and bring the campaign personally to a victorious close. Queen Victoria knew her soldiers would never serve under a Bonaparte. So she begged him not to risk his precious life in the Crimea.

The Windsor visit was a diplomatic success and a return trip to Paris was paid that autumn, the first by an English sovereign since the baby Henry VI was crowned there in 1431. Victoria revelled in the lovely city. At Windsor she had bespattered her white tulle ball gown with Albert's favourite flower, convolvulus, and at St Cloud she covered herself with geraniums, as if she were one of Sir Joseph Paxton's famous conservatories. The Parisians giggled at her short, stout figure, as against the Empress Eugénie's graceful height; but when it came to sitting down at the opera after standing for applause, the audience noticed that the Queen sat straight down without first looking behind her, while Eugénie looked back to make sure there was a chair to receive her. Victoria was born to be a queen.

Poor Albert's weak stomach was a casualty of the rich French *cuisine*, and hostile critics added that Victoria fell for the Emperor because he was the first man who had made love to her. This was not true. Napoleon III belonged to the *outrè* type of adventurer whose flirtatiousness amused her. She had met it before in the Duke of Brunswick at Kensington and would meet it again in Disraeli.

After Paris, Balmoral. Fortunately a major event occurred to give peaceful Balmoral the romance it was in danger of losing to Paris. Sebastopol fell at last to the French on 10 September 1855. There was wild dancing round the bonfire on the old cairn with plenty of whisky. The Treaty of Paris was signed on 2 February 1856 and the Crimean War ended with the Peace of Paris on 3 March, but Queen Victoria felt far from satisfied. She had called it an unsatisfactory war on its outbreak, and unsatisfactory it remained at its conclusion. Queen and country would have preferred it to be hungry, ill-kempt British soldiers with their moustaches frozen over their lips, who first seized Sebastopol, instead of the better fed and cared for French.

Of the people who caught her attention during the two years of hostilities, probably the most satisfactory was a woman:

Florence Nightingale, of whom the Queen actually wrote, 'I envy her', because her sick and wounded soldiers at her Scutari base showered her with fruit and flowers when she too caught the fever. It was said that her influence could save poor drunken soldiers from the bottle. (And she was good enough to say that Her Majesty's influence could do the same.) A time would come when Her Majesty would say, 'If only they had Miss Nightingale at the War Office!' And yet this was the same Queen Victoria who had written, after rightly extolling Albert's spectacular part in the Great Exhibition, 'We women are not made to govern.' She was about to find that sometimes women *must* govern.

FOUR

DEATH COMES FOR ALBERT, 1857–61

The years leading up to the marriage of Vicky, the Princess Royal, to Fritz, Prince of Prussia, in January 1858, caused Queen Victoria to take a step forward in her personal development and in her relations with Prince Albert. The first problem that aroused her energies was Vicky's growing up. The Queen's reactions were typically contradictory.

Vicky became engaged to Fritz on a Balmoral mountain at the age of fourteen. Of course her mother knew perfectly well that Vicky was still only a child – and indeed her parents had previously decided that she could not marry until she was a woman, namely, at the towering age of seventeen. The Queen's conscience told her that she should not promote this child-marriage, deeply in love though little Vicky was with her tall, moustached Fritz. Therefore Vicky could not be a child: woman she had to be, despite her childish waddling walk, her gobbling at meals and laughing far too loud. To prove how mature she really was, the Queen sent Fritz's mother an astonishing letter, detailing Vicky's early, painless steps to puberty.

Why did Vicky's parents set up this dilemma to torment themselves with, for Albert also suffered in his own way? He adored his clever eldest child and an early parting was the last thing he really wanted. Moreover, though he successfully trained Vicky in politics for an hour every evening, he was unable to guide her on more intimate subjects: according to the accepted morality, no unmarried girl could talk intimately to a man, even her father.

The Queen was punishing herself in yet another way by agreeing to this disguised child-marriage: now that Vicky was a woman, she had to sit up with her parents for dinner, instead of going to bed after supper with her siblings. This was agony for the Queen, much as she loved her daughter. She had come to look forward passionately to dinner alone with Albert. More and more during the day he was absent on business. But at dinner she had always had him to herself. Now it was '*diner à trois*'. So why did they agree to the match? The answer is that it was a marriage of political convenience. Fritz, among the most eligible Protestant princes in Europe, would one day soon become King of Prussia after his uncle, the present King, died. One of Albert's favourite phrases was '*Ich habe einen Plan*' – 'I have a plan'. He used it about his children's education, his royal residences, the welfare of artisans, the Queen's future improvement. He was always planning. But this time it was a plan of huge proportions, enveloping the whole of unregenerate Europe. Through his clever daughter, Albert intended to reform the political ideas and methods of the Prussians. Through Fritz, Prussia would be a new power in Europe standing for constitutional government. The Prussian Chancellor, Count Bismarck, called the Coburgs 'the stud-farm of Europe'. The joke would be that after Albert's planning the stud-farm would breed ideas as well as babies, and would operate from a pulpit. (Another joke was that when Vicky was taken to see constitutional government at work in the House of Commons, she found Gladstone and Disraeli having a slanging match.) In any case, if her parents waited until the little catalyst was genuinely grown-up, they would risk losing Fritz to someone else.

The Queen's final preparations showed her battling or negotiating with what Albert called 'the outside world' to some effect. Asking Parliament for Vicky's dowry – a task she had dreaded – produced an acceptable comprise: out of the £80,000 Victoria suggested, Parliament granted £40,000. Her contradictory mixture of personal grandeur and simplicity was well illustrated by two other nuptial events. Vicky's future in-laws tactlessly proposed that the bride should be dispatched to Prussia to be married there. The outraged Queen delivered a broadside through Lord Clarendon, her foreign secretary, that has caused pleasure and amusement ever since it was published in her *Letters*: '. . . the assumption of its being *too much*' she wrote on 25 October 1857, 'for a Prince Royal of Prussia *to come* over to marry *the Princess Royal of Great Britain* IN England is too absurd. . . . it is not *every* day that one marries the eldest daughter of the Queen of England.'[1] This *hauteur* was balanced by the Queen of England's amazingly mixed attire at the grand party given for the Prussians before the wedding: to balance her parure of magnificent diamonds she decorated her hair with wild flowers and grass.

After the wedding on 25 January and a short honeymoon, the young couple left for Germany on 2 February, the small figure of Vicky wrapped in white velour to match the snowflakes falling outside. Albert had to watch a great display of emotion from his family, instead of the self-control he preached – his wife cried bitterly and thought of a poor lamb being led to the slaughter, while all Vicky's sisters and brothers sobbed aloud.

Vicky's marriage was to spark off more than one scene between her parents. It must be emphasised, however, that these scenes were not a proof of Albert's faltering love for Victoria, though some writers have said so. The occasional coldness that sometimes seems to sound through the numerous notes and even 'certificates of improvement' he wrote to her was entirely due to the schoolmasterly manner he would adopt for the purpose of 'improving' her. Albert was incurably pedagogic. There were indeed emotional moments, as we shall see, when the Prince showed his feelings with a long embrace. On the whole, however, it was not his love that Victoria wanted to be reassured about but his approval. She had two personal passions during these years: the passion for Albert and the passion for self-improvement. And they were inextricably entwined. It was through Albert, and through Albert alone, that she felt the necessary improvement came within her reach.

Whatever took him away from her – whether it was the Horticultural Society or bus-loads of philosophers at Balmoral, or, for a short period, Vicky's involuntary intrusion into their *diner à deux* – she resented. Whatever brought him closer – walks together, games with the babies, their double desk-work at Osborne – was welcome. And so the certificate of improvement, that might sound to outsiders like an uninspiring end-of-term report, was to her a wonderful love-letter.

Sir James Clark, her old Court doctor, was one friend who would have agreed with her on the importance of Albert's influence, though he tended to give her thesis a doubtful twist, being always over-impressed with the Queen's descent from her 'mad' grandfather, George III. Clark had written in his diary as early as 5 and 15 February 1856, 'Regarding the Queen's mind: the time will come when she will be in danger [he meant her change of life]. . . . Much depends on the Prince's management. . . . If I could impress him with what I consider necessary I should almost consider the Queen safe.'[2] What Clark considered necessary was for the Prince to keep her both 'quiet' and 'amused'. The Prince must have known about the old King's malady, and also about Clark's views. Fortunately Albert took the opposite line to Clark, urging his wife to get out of herself and live in the real world. For Clark's mental diagnosis was coloured by an event – the menopause – that was much further away than he expected. The Queen was not yet forty; she was to have yet another child most successfully and would still be capable of child-bearing at the age of fifty. Meanwhile the scenes, the analytical notes and the deep love beneath it all continued between Victoria and Albert.

One reason why the Queen dismissed 1856 as a 'gloomy' year was that from August onwards she was in the early stages of her ninth and last pregnancy. She did not accept Albert's solution to the loneliness she felt when he was away – that she could enjoy the company of her eight children instead. She answered that owing to her strange childhood, spent among adults, she had never acquired the taste for adolescent company and conversation. It is ironical to note that after Albert's death the Queen's friends recommended her children's companionship as a substitute for his, with the same result. Yet after the birth of Princess Beatrice on 14 April 1857, the Queen felt better and stronger than ever before, and her wedding anniversary of 10 February was happier than ever.

Just over two months after the birth of 'Baby', the Queen was able to bestow further pleasure on Albert. With Palmerston's support on 25 June 1857 by letters patent she granted Albert the title of Prince Consort.

There was no black depression after Beatrice's birth, as had been the case with most of the children. Indeed the Queen received the grim news of the Indian Mutiny and Cawnpore massacre with the kind of constructive objectivity the Prince Consort was always demanding. When India was transferred from the East India Company to the Crown, a wave of maternal feeling swept over her. She redrafted the Proclamation from the Crown until it was more like a caring female sovereign speaking to her Indian peoples than a mere ruler. The queen's new relations with her peoples were to bear important fruit after the Prince Consort was no longer there to applaud.

Meanwhile, Napoleon III gave Albert and Victoria significant trouble. He had been nicknamed 'Annexander' by their Uncle Leopold, King of the Belgians, after the French defeated Austria at Solferino in 1858, backed Italy, and annexed Savoy and Nice. Lord Russell had also always backed Italy's campaign for freedom. But the Prince Consort remained loyal to Austria's empire, and all empires, nicknaming Russell 'the Old Italian Master'. To cheer the Queen he took her in his arms. The date was 13 December 1860 – almost exactly one year before she was taking his cold hands in hers.

The only subject on which the royal pair still sparred was Vicky. Her mother had hoped she would wait a year or two before starting a family, but no, her son Prince William was born on 27 January 1859 after a terrible labour resulting in a breach birth and dislocation of the baby's left arm.

Throughout the pregnancy her mother had inundated Vicky with well-meaning letters of advice. Vicky's less frequent replies were manna to the Queen. By the time Vicky was a mother (and set to produce a second child – Princess Charlotte – almost at once) Queen Victoria knew more about her own views on sex than she had gathered over the whole of her earlier life. When Vicky wrote exaltedly about the wonder of creating a new human being, Queen Victoria replied: 'What you say of the pride of giving life to an immortal soul is very fine, dear, but . . . I think much more of our being like a cow or a dog at such moments when our poor nature becomes so very animal & unecstatic . . .'[3] Victoria had always found babies frog-like rather than beautiful; now their mothers, when pregnant or in labour, also belonged to the animal world. When Albert snubbed her for tiring Vicky with her letters, she rounded on man as lover and father. 'That despising our poor degraded sex (for what else is it as we poor creatures are born for man's pleasure and amusement . . .) is a little in all clever men's natures; dear Papa even is not quite exempt . . .'[4] It was a relief that Vicky had at least given her sister Alice a slight healthy horror of marriage.

Thus we see the beginning of the greatest contradiction of all in Queen Victoria's amazingly paradoxical character: her husband was her life, yet she would have grasped the essence of late Victorian attacks on the home – 'Home is the girl's prison', wrote Bernard Shaw. And who would write that there was too much marrying these days? Not Bernard Shaw, but Queen Victoria.

As more and more of the royal children reached adolescence, the Prince would repeat with increasing conviction: 'Ich habe einen Plan.' His plan for the young Prince of Wales was the only one that failed completely. It was based on counteracting what his mother believed to be her own Hanoverian weaknesses, magnified in Bertie into a caricature of herself: the frivolity, the self-indulgence, the lack, as yet, of any taste for self-improvement. Well aware of Bertie's devotion to his brother Affie, their

parents unwisely separated them, consigning the unlucky Bertie
to the care of a tedious tutor. When Bertie showed an interest
in Wellington, writing a promising essay on him as a hero, Mr
Gibbs made Bertie write about Hannibal, in whom the Prince
of Wales had less than no interest. A doomed 'plan' by his
father to thin Bertie's all-too royal blood consisted in as boring
a diet as possible, based on seltzer water. It was scarcely
surprising that when Bertie escaped into the army, he enjoyed
the companionship of the actress Nellie Clifton, inveigled into
his bed by his humorous friends at the Curragh Camp, Dublin.

It is doubtful whether Bertie had any very clear idea of what
was going on. His parents never attempted to have the facts of
life elucidated for him and in his later teens he had himself put
some hesitant questions to a volunteer counsellor. But the
notorious Curragh incident of autumn 1861 would probably
have borne no fruit, good or bad, had not the busybody
Stockmar, interfered. In many ways the royal family owed much
to the loyal, intelligent baron. But on two points he did real
harm. First, he persuaded Victoria and Albert that the English
sovereign was a kind of permanent prime minister, dominating
the party system – not the way to present nascent democracy to
a nineteenth-century queen. Second, he sent Albert an alarmist
letter about Bertie's escapade. Without that letter the Curragh
episode might have blown over without Victoria and Albert
knowing anything about it, for there was no blackmail by Nellie,
as Albert feared. Without that letter Victoria would not have
seen Albert's woebegone face on 12 November 1861, the day it
arrived and the day Albert drafted a reproachful but forgiving
appeal to Bertie. Nor would she have dreamed up the nightmare
scenario by which Bertie virtually destroyed his father by
breaking his heart.

Christmas 1860 was the happiest ever, with the present tables, the decorated trees and dearest Albert at the heart of everything. But Albert had not got satisfactorily through his first serious physical test. It came on 1 October 1860 during a visit to his beloved Coburg. He was forced to jump from his runaway carriage before it crashed at a level-crossing. The Queen was informed that it was a minor accident, but he had suffered concussion and wept to his brother Ernest that he would never see Coburg again. Stockmar's contribution was to predict that if he ever contracted something dangerous, he would not fight it. Nevertheless the anniversary of their wedding-day, 10 February, came around again in 1861 to the high hopes of the Queen: she expected a new epoch of 'improvement' to begin, as it had in April 1857 after 'Baby' was born.

Yet in 1861 Albert was visibly deteriorating. At just over forty his hair was going and his weight increasing, while he often looked ill and fagged or went down with catarrh, rheumatism or feverish gastric attacks. And as early as the 1850s his weak stomach had come to stay. The Queen put it down to overwork. But what would happen when Fritz's uncle died and their little Vicky became ruler of Prussia? In emergencies, or when required, Albert would be the 'uncrowned king' twice over – of England and Prussia – with a doubled workload.

And death kept striking their friends and family. Sir James Clark's successor, the bright young Dr William Baly, was killed in a rail accident at Wimbledon, the only passenger to die, as the Queen pointed out characteristically to a neglectful Providence. Then on 16 March 1861 the Duchess of Kent, now Victoria's *beloved* Mama, died of cancer at Frogmore in Windsor. After the coming of her nephew Albert, the Duchess had been integrated into the tribe, with special reference to her grandchildren. She was the first to spot that little Leo's continual falls, bruising and bleeding were something special, in fact haemophilia. When the Queen had asked Mama how to deal with Leo's self-destructive wilfulness, 'Whip him well?' — the Duchess had replied that she could not bear to hear a child cry. 'But when you had *eight* . . .'

Partly due to guilt, after her mother's death the Queen had a breakdown. Mama's diary showed that far from being Conroy's lover, she had doted on the little Victoria all along; yet Queen Victoria still spoke of her childhood as unloved. Her breakdown gave Lord Clarendon his chance to write one of his favourite letters to the beloved Duchess of Manchester. The Queen, if not mad, was on the brink.

And Vicky heard on the Berlin grapevine that her mother was attended by all the doctors in Europe.

It was at Balmoral that Albert was able to restore her happiness and cap it with an optimistic certificate. On 22 October he added to a 'very good certificate' of improvement the promise to help the Queen control her grief: 'controlling your feeling is your great task, you say, in life.'[5]

The last sermon the Prince Consort ever heard at Balmoral began with the text, 'Prepare to meet thy God.' This was intended to be a joyful salute to the Duchess of Kent, lately in a better world; but if Napoleon III with his passion for the occult had been in the Highlands with the unhealthy-looking young Prince, he would have known what to think.

That autumn Albert explained to Victoria that his happy life would not prevent him letting go if struck by a severe illness, while she would cling on. Albert was probably echoing Stockmar's remarks made after his carriage crash in Coburg. By 12 November, two other Coburg royals had failed to cling on:

the Portuguese royal family was struck by an epidemic of typhoid. Both King Pedro, aged twenty-five, and his brother Prince Ferdinand were beloved of Albert and shared the Coburg melancholy; Pedro was like a son to him. Afterwards the Prince Consort worked out that in the ten days from 12 to 22 November he was sickening for typhoid (incubating). By the 22nd he was suffering from chills and insomnia (a typhoid symptom) but he still forced himself to accompany the Queen when inspecting 200 Eton Volunteers. This was not a good day for Stockmar's news of Bertie's indiscretion to arrive. Would it prevent Bertie's courtship of Princess Alexandra of Denmark, as planned by his parents? *Ich habe einen Plan* – for the last time . . .

On Sunday 1 December Albert showed himself an Uncrowned King yet again. In the cold early morning, wrapped in his dressing-gown, he redrafted for Foreign Secretary Russell a bellicose dispatch to the United States in a more conciliatory form. The Confederates (South) had sent two emissaries, plus wives – Mr and Mrs Mason and Mr and Mrs Sliddell – on a British ship, the *Trent*, to seek British support in the American War. They were chased and kidnapped at sea by their opponents. Albert's magic with a pen he could scarcely hold changed an ultimatum into an acceptable plan for negotiation. And the Confederates' documents on board? Mrs Sliddell had saved them by stuffing them into her crinoline.

By now the Prince was too weak to hold a pen, as he said, but too restless to stay in bed and too much deprived of professional nursing care to get his illness under control. Wandering, literally, from room to room with the distraught Queen following him, he also wandered in his mind, believing he was back at the Rosenau when he heard the birds at Windsor. His only nurses were his valet and equerries.

It was not till the end of the first week in December that the Queen's doctors stopped playing the psychological game and told her that Albert had 'low fever'. Low fever, slow fever, gastric fever or bowel fever – they were all euphemisms for the dreaded typhoid. What line to take, however, may well have puzzled the doctors. Albert had always insisted that a fever would kill him; on Friday 13 December Victoria was writing in her journal: 'I prayed & cried as if I should go mad. *Oh!* that I was not then & there crazed! I can't attempt description for he was my Life!' But now the game was up. Albert had told Alice that he was dying, and she had to warn Vicky of the truth.

By six on the morning of Saturday 14 December the wheel had come full circle and the Albert Victoria saw lying in the Blue Room was the same Albert she had first fallen in love with. She used the same word, 'beautiful'. 'Never can I forget how beautiful my Darling looked . . . .'[6] The poor Queen needed a breath of air and was allowed out for half an hour. But she could hear a military band playing at a distance. The sound of the trumpets was too poignant and she had to return indoors. Perhaps she heard all the trumpets sounding for him on the other side. Yet a chorale played at a distance by Princess Alice had comforted her father as he lay dying.

* * *

What did the Prince Consort die of? Daphne Bennett was the first, among several important historians, to suggest that the killer was not typhoid. In an excellent Appendix to her *King Without a Crown – Albert Prince Consort of Great Britain 1819–1861* she gives her reasons. Impressed but not convinced, I offer replies to her main arguments. First, Bennett says there was no typhoid epidemic, nor any information as to where the Prince's infection came from. True, but at this particular date the whole of England was in a sense suffering from a permanent fever epidemic. In 1865, just before the first Public Health Act, one man in three was dying of fever. Prince Albert was surely among them. He had had to come in from a pleasure-trip on the River Thames with the Queen because of the appalling stink. Bennett adds that there was no delirium in Albert's case, no real weakness for he went on dressing, walking about and getting out of bed. She cautiously puts forward instead a cancer, hepatitis or renal failure as the cause of his death. But the Queen's journal does mention delirium. And why should Dr William Jenner, the Queen's new doctor and a specialist on typhoid and typhus, have allowed the Prince to imagine he had typhoid if in fact he did not? It was the one illness about which the Prince was slightly paranoid. His constitution was never robust and it would have been easy to forget cancer, etc. and say the trouble was general exhaustion from overwork. There was no need for the great typhoid expert to invent the presence of the one enemy who would win.

On the evening of 14 December the Prince Consort began to sink rapidly. The Prince of Wales had been sent for from Cambridge, but in such discreet language that he fulfilled an engagement before starting. The Prince Consort's bed, now in the small Blue Room, was pushed out from the wall to allow his children to kiss his hands and say goodbye. The Queen, who had been sent to lie down next door, was fetched back. She asked for 'ein Kuss' and he moved his lips.

It should be noted that the Queen had asked for a last 'kuss' and not a last kiss. In fact, as the Prince lost and regained consciousness at intervals, he made his final brief return not to life in England but to youth in Coburg. 'Wer ist das?' he asked in one unseeing moment and the Queen replied, 'Es ist das kleinen Frauchen.'[7] His 'little wife' realised that he was dying in German and in a sense in Germany. This leads on to a second interesting fact. Whereas Vicky's marriage was intended in a certain respect to anglicise Germany, *en revanche*, the best of Germany – its hard work and seriousness – took possession of Victoria through Albert.

This writer has for long believed that Lytton Strachey's account of Prince Albert's death, particularly the Queen's dramatic reaction to it, was a mixture of intelligent guesswork and vivid imagination. His only original sources were Greville's diaries. It is quite impossible that Strachey should have seen the Queen's journals, which were made accessible only to much later writers like James Pope-Hennessy and myself. Then how did Strachey get it right? For it is to Strachey that we owe the first echo of her wild cry, as she realised that her Prince was dead: a cry totally out of keeping with the dignified image of the late-Victorian Queen-Empress, a paragon of self-control, both unamused and untormented.

'She shrieked – one long wild shriek', wrote Strachey,[8] 'that rang through the terror-stricken Castle . . . she had lost him for ever'. Up till the 1960s I assumed that Strachey had got it wrong, inventing the 'wild shriek' to satisfy his own Gothic imagination. (The 'terror-stricken Castle' may well be Gothic.) Then how did Strachey get it so nearly right? Surely he is reflecting a legend? A legend that had haunted the Castle for half a century. The legend of a great love, a great happiness, a memorable marriage, all ending in a wild shriek. It is the stuff of which legends are made, and there were enough courtiers and family present to give it authority.

Queen Victoria herself could not face describing it in her journal until eleven years later, though she made two earlier attempts and kept notes. Meanwhile the legend of her undying love, expressed in a broken-hearted cry, was born, and was ready to give the lie to that other legend of her mindless, even insane, seclusion. However, at last in 1872 she came to describe that central event of 14 December 1861, indeed the central event of her life: 'Two or three long but perfectly gentle breaths were drawn, the hand clasping mine . . . *and all all* was over, . . . I stood up, kissing his dear heavening forehead & called out in a bitter agonising crying: "Oh! my dear Darling!" & then dropped on my knees in muted, distracted dispair, unable to utter a word or shed a tear!'[9]

FIVE

SECLUSION, 1861–9

What was Prince Albert's main bequest to the nation he had left so prematurely? Undoubtedly it was Queen Victoria, Improved Version. Of course there were many groups of human beings who owed much to their forward-looking Prince Consort – artisans, labourers, scientists, horticulturalists, artists. Some of them named him Albert the Good; others blessed him for the great museum complex at South Kensington, later to become 'Albertopolis'; others again felt his generally benign influence as expressed in the gilded figure of the Albert Memorial, seated opposite the Albert Hall. But for sheer value to the whole nation, caught in mid-century without a male consort, the Improved Victoria was incomparable.

Three ways in which Albert improved Victoria immediately spring to mind. First, he largely succeeded in taming Victoria's self-will, part of her Hanoverian inheritance, but exaggerated by her very abnormal childhood. Second, a positive attitude towards social and constitutional reform was adopted by the Queen – provided there was not too strong a demand for it! In that case reform became revolution, provoked by agitators. Third, she discovered in herself a genuine need for the company of clever people, whereas in pre-Albert days her self-confidence was too weak for her to risk conversation with intellectuals.

True, in a few ways Albert's death damaged Victoria more than his life had improved her. The Blue Room in which he died got frozen into a static tribute to grief. Nothing could ever be changed, and it was carefully photographed to prevent such a possibility. The dread of domestic change entered the Queen in other, more serious ways. She could not bear changes in the personnel of the royal household. This was awkward when a lady-in-waiting wanted to get married and for a widow at Court to remarry was considered by Her Majesty unnecessary if not immoral. Yet so complex and contradictory was the Queen's nature that when it came to Prince Albert's burial his last resting-place – the new Royal Mausoleum at Frogmore – reversed most nineteenth-century ideas of death. It was as bright and beautiful as the Queen could make it. She could have had him laid under the dark floor of St George's Chapel, Windsor, along with her own ancestors but she would not.

The saddest effect of the Prince's death was her seclusion. Her natural need for a period of grieving – modern drugs and counselling would have helped – turned at times into something paranoid and was referred to frankly in the royal journals as 'my seclusion', as if it were some kind of religious vocation. In reality it was that part of her temperament that longed for a quiet, simple life, now having an excuse to take over and become an obsession. She had vowed never to depart from dearest Albert's precepts. But by her seclusion she was breaking one of his most insistent commands: to mix more with the outside world.

Her family suffered the loss of their father and of the cheerful home they had known. Princess Alice was married to Prince Louis of Hesse-Darmstadt in July 1862. As her mother gloomily said, it was 'still December', the month of blessed Papa's death: Alice's wedding might just as well have been her funeral.

Seclusion was Queen Victoria's drug, and it had a physical effect, as drugs do. She lost weight, suffered from headaches and – most unexpected – could not bear the cold. It had always been her boast, and was to be so again, that when others shivered she flourished. No longer. She had lost the will to live, and indeed neither expected nor wished to outlive her husband by more than one year. She prayed to follow Albert. But this led to one of the many contradictions in her life and character. Bertie's 'fall' at the Curragh Camp may, in his mother's opinion, have broken his father's heart and so led to his death. The thought of that fall still made her shudder. Not everyone, she realised, would understand that shudder. None of her ministers would understand, except Mr Gladstone. But in view of that shudder, and its cause, the Prince of Wales was clearly not yet fit to wear the Crown. So she prayed to God to let her live on. Perhaps it was fortunate that it was left to God, rather than to man, to sort out her contradictory prayers.

Actually, Albert's plans for Bertie's future were well advanced when he died and despite his fears that Bertie's fall would lose him his preferred bride, Bertie and Princess Alexandra of Denmark were married at St George's Chapel, Windsor, on 5 March 1863. The wedding was of interest for various reasons. It was a test for the Queen's seclusion, a test that she passed with noted success even though she described herself to her old Uncle Leopold as a poor hunted hare. In fact she concealed herself during the ceremony in Catherine of Aragon's Closet, well above the altar and bridal couple. When Mr Disraeli tried to quiz her through his glass, the poor hunted hare gave him a look he was not meant to forget. After the ceremony Her Majesty retired to the peaceful, gaslit mausoleum at Frogmore, leaving her guests to battle their way home by overcrowded special train, Disraeli sitting on his wife Mary Ann's lap.

But if there was still any doubt whether this poor hare was the hunter or the hunted, it was cleared up by the episode of Prince Alfred at Malta. A dashing young naval officer, Affie had got into a scrape with a lady. The Queen was on to it.

The younger generation at the Wales wedding was also beginning to attract attention. The Queen's fifth and youngest daughter, Princess Beatrice, aged nearly six, was thrilled to be driven through the town of Windsor and amazed to discover 'there was *stays* in shops'. Her nephew, little Prince William of Prussia, eldest of all the Queen's grandchildren, threw Aunt Beatrice's muff out of the carriage window, before biting his young, kilted uncle's bare knees in the Chapel. Beatrice was to remain an amusing and William an aggressive child, though he called his gloomy grandmother 'Duck'.

Princess Alexandra, the bride, had been told to say that the new bond between Denmark and England had no political significance. But Prince Albert should have been there to handle the changes it in fact brought about. In that same year, 1863, Europe was divided over the complicated Schleswig-Holstein affair and Queen Victoria now found herself with a child in each hostile camp: Vicky naturally supporting Prussia's claims to the Duchies, Bertie backing Denmark's, while the Queen was to sympathise with good old Fritz Holstein's claim for independence. No one in England really seemed to know which claimant was right, if any, and a popular witticism circulated to the effect that only three people understood the Schleswig-Holstein problem: Prince Albert, and he was dead; a German professor, and he had gone mad; and Melbourne, and he had forgotten. A variant of the above said that only God knew and He wouldn't say.

And so from this basis of non-understanding or misunderstanding, Queen Victoria faced a Europe fuller than ever of her kith and kin – and at war. Only one person knew his own mind thoroughly and had the power and ruthlessness to give his ambitions effect: Chancellor Bismarck of Prussia. In 1864 Prussia invaded the Duchies, afterwards sharing the spoils of war with Austria, which in due course Prussia then defeated at Sadowa. Prince Albert had already given Queen Victoria the watchword of neutrality, which worked well with British ministers but was uncomfortable with the family.

About the same time came the second rude reaction to the Queen's seclusion – the first being Dizzy's quizzing-glass. Anonymous insulting notices appeared outside Buckingham Palace: 'These commanding premises to be let or sold, in consequence of the late occupant's declining business.' And on 1 April *The Times* laughingly lied that Her Majesty was about to 'break her protracted seclusion'. Her Majesty decided it was time for her to appear on her first public carriage drive since beloved Albert's death. Though she did not mention it in her journal, there was always a danger that, while low-born subjects were very occasionally rude, high-born beings from Society might begin imputing more sinister reasons for her seclusion; in point of fact Lord Clarendon had thought that 'Eliza' (his nickname for Victoria in his letters to the notorious Duchess of Manchester) had been getting madder and madder ever since her mother's death. During that first carriage drive the Queen noted without displeasure how loudly the good people cheered her compared with the Waleses. Mild jealousy was a useful force in drawing Her Majesty out of seclusion.

Three deaths in the early 1860s removed more of the pillars on which Victoria had leaned, and taught her to stand on her own feet. Baron Stockmar died in 1863. When the letters she had written to him were returned, she was surprised to find how full they were of Albert's 'poor dear stomach'. How did she react to this discovery? For once she did not confide her innermost thoughts to her journal; perhaps because they were not entirely loyal to the vision of blessed Albert's perfection. She had had to learn to manage with less of poor dear Albert's help for years, rather than days before he died.

On 18 October 1865 she lost yet another link with Albert and the past. Lord Palmerston died. In her opinion he was a model of will, intelligence and courage. He may have backed the wrong horse in Europe – Italian freedom from Austria – but he was the first minister to recognise her as Head of State by telling her *everything*. Then came the final blow to her habits of dependency: the death of her confidant Uncle Leopold, King of the Belgians, on 10 December 1865, just four days before the sacred Mausoleum Day itself. As Princess Alice said to dear Mama, now she was Head of all the Family.

King Leopold had wanted to be buried at Windsor, but the Catholic clergy of Belgium forbade it. 'Nasty "beggars", as Brown would say,' wrote the Queen to the Princess Royal – though it is doubtful whether Brown really bothered to trim his vowel, even in deference to Majesty.

It should be noted that the Queen was already beginning to quote John Brown; and indeed the years around 1865 are some of the most important in assessing the Brown scandal. But it must not be overlooked that another of the Queen's guardian spirits – an entirely benign one – also emerged in precisely this year: her future principal private secretary, Sir Henry Ponsonby. Born into the famous Anglo-Irish family that included Lady Caroline Lamb among others, Captain Ponsonby had been one of Prince Albert's equerries. A strong Liberal in politics married to the lively feminist Mary Bulteel, Henry Ponsonby provided

Queen Victoria with exactly the antidote she needed to the many extreme diehard influences in her court. Among other things Ponsonby kept a balanced view of John Brown, calling him a Child of Nature, rather than a son of Satan, as some of her family and courtiers suspected. It might even be, the gossips hinted, that 'King John' had reduced Queen Victoria to becoming Mrs Brown; Ponsonby knew the Queen's nature too well to imagine that she would ever sleep with a servant.

John Brown was a tall bearded Highlander with a powerful frame and a good mind. Everything that was once believed of John Conroy and the Queen's mother was now being applied to John Brown and the Queen herself. The difference was that whereas Conroy was expelled, Brown died in harness. The first mistake in the popular legend of Brown was to spot him leading the Queen's pony under the Windsor battlements as early as 1862, as if the Queen had only waited for Prince Albert to die before bringing Brown south. In fact Brown was seen at the 1862 Kensington Exhibition with the other gillies, before they all returned together to Balmoral. It was only at the end of 1864, when the Queen's seclusion was well under way, that Dr Jenner suggested Brown should be brought south to entice the unhappy Queen into the fresh air. She felt so 'safe' with Big Brown leading her pony. Thus it was not until 1865 that the Brown position really began to build up.

By February 1865 Brown was a permanent part of the royal household, being known officially as the Queen's Highland servant, with a salary that had started at £120 and rose to £310 a year. At thirty-nine, he was promised a cottage if he got married. His only object, wrote Victoria to her eldest daughter on 5 April, was to take care of his Queen – '& God knows how much I want to be taken care of'. If a tourist at Balmoral

Portrait miniature of Queen Victoria, 1839 (watercolour on enamel on gold), by William
Essex (1784–1869). (Ashmolean Museum/Bridgeman Art Library)

*Her Most Gracious Majesty
Queen Victoria Receiving the
Sacrament at her Coronation.*
(Maidstone Museum and
Art Gallery/Bridgeman Art
Library)

Prince Albert, the Prince
Consort (1819–61) by Franz
Xavier Winterhalter (1806–73)
(studio of). (Philip Mould,
Historical Portraits
Ltd/Bridgeman Art Library)

The marriage of Queen
Victoria and Prince
Albert at St James's Palace,
10 February 1840.
(*The Illustrated London News*)

Osborne House, East Cowes: exterior built in the Italian style for Queen Victoria and
Prince Albert, *c.* 1845–8, by Thomas Cubitt.(John Bethell/Bridgeman Art Library)

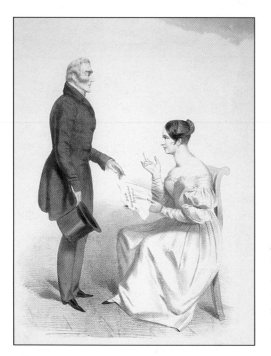

A Cabinet Lecture, Queen
Victoria with Lord
Melbourne, 1840
(engraving, English School,
nineteenth century). (British
Museum/Bridgeman Art
Library)

Queen Victoria distributing the Victoria Cross in Hyde Park, London, 1857. The medal for
valour was instituted the year before. (*The Illustrated London News*)

Queen Victoria on Horseback with John Brown, by Charles Burton Barber (1845–94).
(The FORBES Magazine Collection/Bridgeman Art Library)

Peace with Honour, Queen Victoria and Benjamin Disraeli following the signing of the
Berlin Treaty in 1878. Picture by Theodore Blake Wirgman (1848–1925). (The FORBES
Magazine Collection/Bridgeman Art Library)

William Gladstone in the House
of Commons outlining his plans
for Irish Home Rule, 1886.
(*The Illustrated London News*)

Queen Victoria and Abdul Karim,
'The Munshi' (b. 1863),
photographed *c.* 1894.
(*The Illustrated London News* Picture
Library/Bridgeman Art Library)

The family at Coburg on the wedding day of the Grand Duke and Duchess of Hesse and the Rhine, 19 April 1894. *Seated, left to right*: William II, German Emperor; Queen Victoria; the Empress Frederick; with Princess Beatrice of Saxe-Coburg Gotha and Princess Feodora of Saxe-Meiningen in front. *First standing row, left to right*: Prince Alfred of Saxe-Coburg Gotha; Nicholas, Tsarevich of Russia; Princess Alix of Hesse and the Rhine; Princess Louis of Battenberg; Princess Henry of Prussia; Grand Duchess Vladimir of Russia; the Duchess of Saxe-Coburg Gotha. *Second standing row, left to right*: the Prince of Wales; Princess Henry of Battenberg; Princess Philip of Saxe-Coburg Kohary (*facing her left*); the Duchess of Saxe-Meiningen; Princess Aribert of Anhalt; the Duchess of Connaught. *Two standing rows at back, left to right*: Prince Louis of Battenberg; Grand Duke Paul of Russia, Prince Henry of Battenberg; Prince Philip of Saxe-Coburg Kohary; Count Mensdorff; Grand Duke Serge of Russia; Crown Princess and Crown Prince Ferdinand of Roumania; Grand Duchess Serge of Russia; Grand Duke Vladimir of Russia; the Duke of Connaught; the Duke of Saxe-Coburg Gotha.

Queen Victoria had the Royal Mausoleum at Frogmore built to house her and Albert's remains. It was designed by Professor Ludwig Gruner, the Prince's artistic adviser, and the architect was A.J. Humbert. The tomb was designed by Carlo Marochetti. (The Royal Collection © 1999 Her Majesty Queen Elizabeth II)

accidentally overheard Brown 'taking care of' the Queen in a distinctly familiar way, calling her 'Wumman' and telling her to hold her chin up when he pinned her cloak or she would get pricked — well, was not that just like a child of nature? The poor Queen needed to be surrounded by people who loved her: by Dean Wellesley and Dr Macleod, with their loving hearts, rather than, say, Dean Stanley who seemed cold and of no sex.

By the following year, 1866, the Queen felt her stony misery beginning to abate under the benign influence of congenial companionship. She wondered if she were betraying dearest Albert. Dean Wellesley, after being consulted, told her that her discovery of certain comforters was not betrayal but 'Providential'.[1]

In the months following, the press gleefully took up the question of Her Majesty's comforters. *Punch* published a skit on John Brown's position at Windsor, in a satirical 'Court Circular'. Mister John Brown was said to walk upon the Castle Slopes, to partake of a haggis and to listen to a bagpipe. In the eyes of the *Lausanne Gazette*, all this graciousness could only mean one thing: that Her Majesty had married Mister Brown. From Mrs Melbourne before Albert's arrival, to Mrs Brown after Albert's departure! How angry the Queen would be, wrote Ponsonby to his wife on 1 October 1866, to read that she had married a servant!

An early mistake made by Queen Victoria herself involved setting the family against Brown. In response to Brown's no doubt heart-rending complaints that his new job was running him off his feet and he could not sleep for his aching legs, the Queen commanded the family not to send Brown on unnecessary errands; worse still, she ordered the smoking-room, favourite haunt of Lenchen's husband Prince Christian of

Schleswig-Holstein who smoked nineteen cigars a day, to be closed in future at midnight. This new edict did not endear Brown to the Queen's burly penniless German son-in-law. It was not long before a scurrilous pamphlet appeared in the United States entitled *John Brown's Legs*.

The Queen was satisfied in her own mind that all the malicious gossip about Brown originated in the upper reaches of Society – 'high-born beings', as she was wont to call them with regal sarcasm. But a letter posted to Buckingham Palace and addressed to Her Majesty was clearly written by a loyal subject from the lower orders. It suggested at the end of October 1866 that, while a better Queen than Victoria did not exist, she should abdicate – time for a change. Give the Prince of Wales a chance . . .

At this same period the Queen's youngest children were working up a passionate dislike, not only of Brown but also of Balmoral. There was a whole series of 'Brown rows' at Balmoral in the 1870s, some caused by the allocation of ponies for riding, others quite simply by the whisky bottle. Princess Louise and Prince Leopold egged each other on in their contempt for John Brown and his Highlands. There was the 'Great Knee Row', when an injury to Louise's knee while riding gave the Queen and Brown an excuse to keep the family at Balmoral for many extra weeks, instead of risking further damage to the knee by travelling south. As Louise remarked bitterly, if the journey had been northwards instead, Mama would have packed her on to a train the minute she could move. Young Leopold, always bored at Balmoral and often with injuries of his own due to his haemophilia, revelled in these rows. 'Oh, what a row,' he would write rapturously.

The Balmoral rows ended in November 1870 with a rumour reaching Mary Ponsonby at Windsor that Brown had decided to escape from it all by getting married. 'Who to?' asked Henry. But there was only one possible answer: to Miss Ocklee, one of the Queen's dressers with whom Brown always danced at the gillies' balls. In the end the project fizzled out, perhaps because the Queen could not bear it, or Brown was too grand to marry a dresser, or Miss Ocklee changed her mind, for she married someone in the Steward's department. But whatever the reason for its negation, the rumour of Brown's marriage has important repercussions for the Queen's story. If Brown was contemplating marriage to a dresser in November 1870, he could not have married the Queen in the 1860s as the sensational press had announced.

There is further evidence from Victoria's own writings that she never made a second marriage after the Prince Consort died. In her private journal of May 1870 – her fifty-first birthday – she wrote the plangent words: 'Alone, alone, as it will ever be.' It is unthinkable that a woman of Queen Victoria's truth-loving nature should try to persuade herself that she was 'alone, alone', if in fact she was wedded to a perfectly good second husband. Even more convincing is a passage in her last will and testament. In this fascinating document John Brown appears as a servant, though a very special one, along with her beloved wardrobe maid, Annie Macdonald, and emphatically not beside her husband. Again it is unthinkable that Brown should be mentioned in her will as one of two deceased servants if in fact he was one of two deceased husbands. No, John Brown was never Queen Victoria's husband. But was he in the enjoyment of some special relationship? Be it her lover or at least her medium?

It is safe to say if Brown had been her lover, one or other of her numerous courtiers, equerries, ladies-in-waiting, dressers, 'rubbers', readers or other attendants would at some point have accidentally seen something. People were in and out of her rooms from morning to night. Some of them kept diaries or wrote intimate private letters that were afterwards published. Yet there is never a sudden kiss, clasp or shout of shame or annoyance at an unexpected interruption. At the same time we are asked to believe that for twenty years these two were secret, undiscovered lovers. There is no evidence for such a fantasy and plenty against, founded upon all we know of Queen Victoria's character. It would have made her angry, wrote Ponsonby, to suggest that she had married a servant. To suggest that she had slept with a servant outside marriage would have provoked not merely anger but Traitor's Gate and Tower Green.

To suggest that John Brown had spiritualistic gifts valued by the Queen is another matter, though that too has been wildly exaggerated by partisan lobbies. Queen Victoria is said to have presented Brown with a gold watch at Osborne in recognition of his work as a medium. But she had already presented him with a gold watch for saving her life from a would-be assassin. Why two gold watches? And the psychic watch was engraved as from 'Osborn' – Osborne being misspelt. Surely the Queen would never have passed such an error. (The 'psychic watch' was stolen from the Society of Psychic Research in whose possession it was until the 1960s.)

Nevertheless the nineteenth century was a period of much interest in mediums and spiritualism. Ministers of the Crown, professors, poets, Sir Henry Ponsonby and Princess Louise were either interested or involved. Queen Victoria and Prince Albert tried a bit of table-turning for fun at Osborne in 1853, Victoria putting it down to magnetism; and Louise collected genuine instances of second sight. Victoria probably credited John with second sight. He was a Highlander and the Argylls had it, so why not the Browns?

In 1861 while Albert was at Balmoral for the last time, Brown appeared to have foreseen both the prince's death and the two deaths in the Portuguese royal family from fever. For he told Her Majesty before they set off south that he hoped there would be no deaths in the family that winter. But there is no evidence whatever that the Queen held seances in the Blue Room with Brown for her medium as some have imagined. John Brown was neither Prince Albert's successor in the marriage-bed nor his go-between in the spirit world. However, there was one particular thing in Queen Victoria's set-up between 1861 and 1871 that did seem to render her relations with Brown either sinister or sexy. Her seclusion. If they had been seen regularly in the Park or in public processions, with him on the box, they might both have got away with it. But Brown was part and parcel of that mysterious landscape that furnished her seclusion: the secret dells of Osborne, the hidden lakes of Balmoral, above all the ghostly trappings of the Blue Room with its beds and chairs and tables all unchanged since the death.

The marriage of another of the Queen's daughters – Princess Helena to Prince Christian of Schleswig-Holstein – gave the Queen that little necessary push to open Parliament for the first time since Prince Albert's death. For a royal marriage required an annuity; in other words a begging bowl. At least Parliament must see the hand that was holding it out.

The ceremony took place on 6 February 1866 and was described by the Queen as if she had been Marie-Antoinette on the way to the guillotine. It was 'an *execution*' to which she was 'dragged in *deep mourning*'.[2] Or perhaps she saw herself as Mary

Queen of Scots, for she decided to wear a black cap instead of the crown.

There were many other small steps forward in that same year, some unwelcome, such as a Buckingham Palace breakfast (garden party) and some pleasant, such as visits to women in hospital or prison. The thing she was most enthusiastic about was a tour of Albert's South Kensington Museum (now called the Victoria and Albert) all of which she delighted in though above all she enjoyed the display of china painted by 'ladies or at least women'. She had earlier been touched by the Windsor workhouse, where the ladies – or at least women – were separated from their husbands: 'hard on them'.[3]

Queen Victoria longed to be a second Florence Nightingale, living simply and visiting the poor and sick. But as Queen of England she was threatened by what might be the worst of all upheavals – a second Reform Bill. There was one compensation. John Bright MP, Radical leader of the Reform League, with its demand for manhood suffrage, actually understood her seclusion. At a public meeting in 1866 he defended mourning Majesty in a few poignant and memorable words: 'a woman – be she the Queen of a great realm or be she the wife of one of your labouring men – who can keep alive in her heart a great sorrow for the lost object of her life . . . is not at all likely to be wanting in a great and generous sympathy for you.'[4] The politics of Reform prevented the Queen from paying her usual spring visit to Balmoral in 1866, so she was lent Cliveden, to which she took a staff of ninety-one, including three doctors.

By 1867 the Liberals had fallen and Reform was in the hands of the Tories. When the new Chancellor and Leader of the House, with his black ringlets and conversational style of a novelist, arrived for his first audience, no second sight disclosed to Victoria the fairyland shimmering within her reach. The impression that Benjamin Disraeli made on her was fair.

The Queen was already pressing Reform on the Tories, thus showing the development of her gifts as sovereign since Albert's death. She knew when her people really wanted something and meant to have it. Reform was a case in point. All the respectable classes agreed in wanting the vote for the towns, she said, and therefore this new Tory government must act. It did. A letter from the Queen to the Princess Royal dated 16 December 1867, the year of the Second Reform Bill, showed the changed tone of Victoria's thinking during this critical period when she was preparing to emerge from seclusion. She had little sympathy with the Tory diehards' view of Reform as 'a leap in the dark', that might, however, succeed in dishing the Whigs. Victoria had as yet no wish to dish the Whigs. She still saw herself as spiritually one of them. In her letter to Vicky she foresaw 'a new French Revolution' impending for Britain, unless the upper classes ceased to be frivolous, pleasure-seeking and immoral, the young men being gamblers and the young women 'fast'. The lower classes, in contrast, 'are so intelligent & earn their bread & riches so deservedly that they cannot & ought not to be kept back . . .'.[5] No doubt John Brown had taught her a thing or two about social history.

Disraeli became Tory Prime Minister in January 1868, and the Queen, under the spell of her own new thinking, wrote excitedly that he was 'risen from the people'. Not so. Dizzy's father was a man of letters, neither a 'highborn being' nor 'lower class'. Nevertheless Dizzy was soon delighting Victoria in two ways: he told her every single thing that mattered, which had never been done before, even by Palmerston; and he allowed her to go on holiday abroad while Parliament was still sitting. However, Disraeli was defeated that November. The least the Queen could do was to create his wife Viscountess Beaconsfield.

Disraeli's successor was William Ewart Gladstone. He was 'The People's William', not Victoria's. Mrs Gladstone, his clever wife, spotted what was necessary and urged her husband to make the Queen his 'pet'. But it was no good. For one thing, he addressed her not as a pet but as a public meeting. He had been a Peelite Tory and joined the Liberals in 1859. The Queen already found him 'strange' – did he not support Votes for All? – and a little mad. He was in favour of disestablishing the Protestant church in Ireland – *her* Church, tithes and all – and his motto was, 'My mission is to pacify Ireland.'[6] What was her mission? To be the People's Queen. So when three Fenians were hanged in Manchester she was able to write in her journal for 23 November 1867, 'I prayed for those poor men last night.' But the two People's Champions, Gladstone and the Queen, got no closer as the months passed. On 25 September 1869 she complained to Vicky of Gladstone's 'want of foresight and sudden enthusiasms' and, as she had already said, 'he talks so very much' – unlike Disraeli whose 'large ideas' were not spoilt by long sentences.

In her first years as head of all the family, 1865–9, she had less trouble from Parliament than from her children. The Prince and Princess of Wales met Garibaldi, the Italian people's champion, when he was visiting England; they did not tell Mama. The Queen loved Alix, wishing her to stay with *her* and to go less into society. In other words she was jealous of the way Alix filled the gap made by her own seclusion. She also disapproved of the Wales's 'Marlborough House set' for their racing and gambling. She banned Bertie from seeing the red state boxes because of his temperament and advised him not to go about too much with Prince Alfred.

Of the girls, Vicky made trouble over Louise's engagement to Lord Lorne, heir of the Duke of Argyll, and a 'subject'. Princess Louise was a sculptress and mixed with artists, while Lorne wrote poetry. Could a poet cure a bohemian? Vicky had wanted her sister for one of the Prussian royalties; but what good had these great matches done? Dearest Papa had advocated them, the Queen pointed out, only *before* Prussia had swallowed up everything. This was the Queen's first overt admission that things had moved on since dearest Papa's death.

Gifts among the family created their own trouble area. Princess Alice wanted two pearls a year towards each of her daughters' pearl necklaces. But with pearls at £40 each, how could the Queen do it for each grandchild, as well as trying to complete the unfinished pearl necklaces of Louise and Beatrice? – especially as Vicky and Alice were known to be plotting the end of Mama's seclusion. Alice in particular was both too advanced and too old-fashioned. She attended classes on anatomy, a subject the Queen thought it was better not to know too much about. And she wore herself out by breast-feeding all those big babies, saying that she was saving them from dysentery.

The Queen was more interested in finding dark-haired and dark-eyed princes and princesses for intermarriage with the royal family, for 'that constant blue eyes and fair hair makes the blood so lymphatic'.[7] By lymphatic she meant watery, whereas the blood royal ought to be dark and strong.

The Queen was head of the national family as well as of the royal family. When she read about poor third-class passengers being liable to rail accidents, she suggested brightly that a Rail Director should be made to travel on every train. That would teach them safety rules! Queen Victoria became ever more impressed by the contrast between high-born beings and servants, the rich and the poor, the proud and the humble – and always to the latter's advantage. Who supported their parents in old age? The poor. She dubbed the bad, bullying attitudes of the rich, 'John Bullism'. It was the John Bulls who caused the poison of class wars and foreign wars; the John Browns who were the antidote. Queen Victoria felt that by the end of the 1860s two things had combined to make her present, simple, semi-secluded way of life acceptable to her people: one was John Bright's picture of Majesty in 1866 as the working-man's guardian – as it were, their Florence Nightingale. The other was her publication in 1868 of *Leaves from the Journal of our Life in the Highlands*, the story of the Balmoral idyll shared by herself and Albert.

It was an appeal to the literate, book-loving middle-class and sold 20,000 copies at once. Not all high-born beings welcomed it. Lady Augusta Stanley, a former lady-in-waiting, could find too many footnotes about footmen, as if they were important gentlemen. On the contrary, the Queen felt the book's popularity to be due to the family's having lived on such a friendly footing with their Highlanders.

She celebrated her fiftieth birthday in 1869, expecting to continue through the 1870s in the same way as she had in the 1860s. The challenge was to come not from the gentlemen of England but from political voices inspired by republican movements abroad. Would she come out from the pages of her *Highland Journal* and fight?

ROYAL RENAISSANCE, 1870–86

The most horribly significant event of 1870 – the Franco-Prussian War – was part of the struggle for power in Europe. It seemed peculiarly horrible to Queen Victoria because her sympathies were torn between her two eldest children.

The Prince of Wales tended to sympathise with France in the war, even though France was technically the aggressor. But that was all the result of Bismarck's falseness. The King of Prussia had sent a civil telegram to the Emperor Napoleon III from Ems, where the King was taking the waters. Bismarck removed all the civilities from the now aggressive 'Ems telegram', which became the *casus belli*. France declared war. The Queen at first feared for Vicky and the Prussians. Even as late as the 1870s it seemed impossible to Victoria that a Napoleon should be defeated. After the Prussian victory she mourned for lovely Paris, punished, as she saw it, in an Old Testament fashion for its sins. Indirectly, the French defeat had a profound effect on Victoria's own future.

Napoleon III's abdication as Emperor and the restoration of the French republic inspired the Radical clubs in England to demand Victoria's abdication and the creation of an English republic. What was the use of a secluded monarch they never saw? Gladstone and Ponsonby became seriously alarmed by what they now called 'The Royalty Question'. Gladstone may even have called Her Majesty a 'worm', by analogy, for he likened the possible fall of the monarchy (due supposedly to the Queen's lifestyle) to the deadly gnawing of a great oak's bark by a worm.

As for her own family, the Queen never allowed seclusion to relax the sharp eye she kept on its members, particularly Bertie. In 1870 she was sorely troubled by the influence of the 'fast set' upon Bertie, and his less than moral influence upon the country. The notorious Mordaunt case illustrated her point. When Sir Charles Mordaunt brought a suit for divorce against his wife, the Prince of Wales was subpoenaed and his letters to Lady Mordaunt read in court. Though the letters were palpably innocent, the lady was 'fast' as well as deranged and Bertie's association with her was 'lowering' when he should have been promoting 'high tone'.[1] On the other hand, Bertie had made a great leap forward in the Queen's affections because of his popularity with the 'lower orders'. They all loved him below stairs.

In the following months the Queen found herself embroiled yet again with Vicky over children. No, Mama did not dislike children, specially not pretty ones. What she disliked was marrying for marrying's sake, huge families, noisy children and the horrors of childbirth, in which 'we poor women' were lowered and our animal nature dominated.[2]

1870 was also the year of the first national Education Act. Again Queen Victoria's pleasure was diminished by the behaviour of many children in those days. For there could be too much education, causing children to question authority, including that of their parents. And those parents themselves, right up to within a fortnight of giving birth, would go on dancing and wearing tight dresses without a shawl or scrap of scarf. . . .

Meanwhile the Princess Royal was drafting what was to be known as 'Vicky's famous letter'. It was to be signed by the whole family, was addressed to 'Our Adored Mama and Sovereign' and was intended to draw the Queen's attention to the danger in which her prolonged absence from full public life was placing the monarchy and her family. The Queen's argument had always been that her absences were dictated by the necessities of her health. 'What killed the Prince Consort?' she would ask, and the reply was always 'Overwork'.[3] The trouble was that observers at Balmoral and elsewhere had noted the robust state of the Queen's health; she had actually climbed up Craig Gowan of her own choice by the hard route.

Suddenly, four days after she wrote her letter about overwork, the dreaded ill-health struck. The date was 14 August 1871 and the Queen was at Osborne. She woke up with a sore throat. By the 22nd she was feeling desperately ill. Never since 1835, when she caught typhoid, had she felt so ill. The Scottish surgeon, Lister, lanced her arm in September and she used the carbolic spray he had invented to kill the germs. Life at Balmoral returned to something like normal in that there were the usual 'Brown rows', both Prince Affie and little Princess Charlotte of Prussia refusing to shake hands with him on arrival.

Jenner extracted an apology from *The Times* for attacking the Queen for shamming, when in fact she had been in pain for six weeks. But no one could stop the publication of an anonymous pamphlet, entitled *What Does She Do With It?*, in which the Queen was said to be hoarding her Civil List, hence her seclusion. At last, by the end of September 1871 she was virtually recovered, having lost 2 stone in weight. By 5 November she felt able to go to kirk again, with John Brown's help. And as if to celebrate the royal recovery, in which the Queen looked healthy but somewhat changed, the Liberal MP, Sir Charles Dilke, chose 6 November as the day on which to call on Parliament to depose Victoria and declare a republic. But just as a prolonged bout of illness had saved the Queen from the attacks of the Radicals, so a new and even more serious illness was to rescue the monarchy from even worse danger. The worm gnawing at the bark of the noble oak seemed never able to finish the job.

This time it was a telegram from Sandringham. On 21 November 1871 the Queen knew that the Prince of Wales had typhoid. After the usual high fever and bouts of delirium in which Bertie made some embarrassing predictions about a new reign, luckily incoherent, the plot dramatically changed. On 14 December, of all dates, the Prince took a turn for the better. On 27 February 1872 the Queen was holding a thanksgiving service at St Paul's Cathedral for the heir's recovery. And as if all this were still not enough to dish the republicans, on 28 February a mad youth named O'Connor made the sixth attempt on Queen Victoria's life. Her highland attendant saved her, thus completing the fateful trilogy and ensuring that the monarchy was saved by septicaemia, typhoid fever and John Brown.

By the summer of 1873 the Queen was on relatively good terms with both Liberals and Conservatives. Disraeli of course had the advantage of now being a widower. When he confided to the Queen that returning home at night since his wife's death meant entering 'a homeless home', she knew exactly how he felt. He cheered her with the news that the Conservative Party was in fine fettle, ready to take over at the right moment. But she knew she had to see her Liberal ministers more often than in the past, or they would find ways of managing without her, especially in sending messages to her troops. Even Gladstone had an unexpected success, perhaps because he was clearly on the way out; he kept her to a promise that she would receive the Shah of Persia. She actually wore her Koh-i-noor diamond in response to his blazing gems. If Gladstone's mission was to redeem Ireland, hers was to do good. She felt she had done it when the Shah was seen kissing her photograph on Windsor station. Best to ignore the three wives reported to have been dumped in Europe, and as for the females rumoured to be in his suite . . .

Europe was in fact the area of her chief anxiety, for Affie had become engaged to the Tsar's only daughter Marie. What a pity she was not the Empress of India, to match the Empress of Russia. They did not treat her quite rightly. Fancy the Russian Empress inviting her to run over to Cologne to meet her new in-laws! In a passion of jealousy and outraged dignity she pointed out to her daughter Alice that she was a reigning monarch and 'Doyenne of Sovereigns', not 'any little Princess ready to run to the slightest call of the *mighty Russians* . . .'[4]

On 10 February 1874 the Queen recorded two moving facts in her journal: it was the thirty-fourth anniversary of her wedding day, and Disraeli was in power again with the first healthy Tory majority since that of Sir Robert Peel. And though she did not yet know it, a new character was about to enter the annals of British history: a Faery Queen.

It is a reflection on the inconsistencies as well as richness of Queen Victoria's character that two such opposite admirers as John Brown and Benjamin Disraeli should have brought about her renaissance: the one 'a coarse animal' when handling the Queen at Balmoral balls, according to a courtier; the other a unique combination of literary imagination and political understanding. When he called Victoria a Faery Queen he did not mean 'faery' as fay but 'faery' as magical. Disraeli's famous letter to his friend Lady Bradford describing Queen Victoria at Osborne, brings out the magical quality while keeping the overall effect suitably down to earth. 'She was wreathed with smiles and, as she tattled, glided about the room like a bird. (Or like a plump Victorian fairy.)' Disraeli half expected to be kissed. Instead he was given a seat, an even greater privilege. In his conquest of the Faery, Disraeli's task was made easier by his predecessor's abject failure. Disraeli noticed that Gladstone treated the Queen like 'a public department' whereas he himself handled her entirely as a woman. The truth was – as Gladstone saw – that the monarch had indeed become in some sense a public department, but not necessarily one that was usually in the wrong and always needed a good talking to. Disraeli was to add, significantly, to Lord Esher, apropos his relations with the Queen: 'I never deny, I never contradict, I sometimes forget . . .'[5]

Possibly his first success with Her Majesty was due to a touch of 'forgetfulness'. He actually got her to leave Balmoral and come south two days early, for the sake of business. We can imagine the Queen announcing her departure date: no argument, no questioning, but somehow everything began to happen just two days earlier. Nevertheless the amusing cynicism of Disraeli's remarks to Esher must not blind us to the fact that quite simply, in the long run, Queen Victoria conquered her Prime Minister. When shaken by asthma, gout and a tiff with Majesty, he was to put it all in one sentence: 'I love the Queen – perhaps the only person left to me in this world that I do love . . .'[6]

There was one new Act of Parliament over which Disraeli had no need to humour the Queen, nor did he need to be chivvied or harried by her. This was the Royal Titles Bill, introduced in 1873 to a critical Parliament and destined for a rough passage. However, on May Day 1876 Queen Victoria was declared Queen-Empress – Empress of India only and Queen as before of Great Britain and Ireland. The Queen's motives were roughly three in launching this innovation. First, the Imperial title would be her contribution to the country's 'high tone'. The Liberals were lowering it; she would raise it. (Disraeli did not warn her of the Bill's likely rough passage. It was better that the Faery Queen should see for herself the limits of the people's enthusiasm for a Faery Empress. Such a magical creature existed in India but nowhere else.) The Queen's next two motives were both personal. Above all there was her rivalry with the European potentates, particularly the Emperor of Russia. There had already been that tiff over a visit to her in-laws at Cologne; how could a reigning monarch pack up in a day? Now there was trouble over the precedence of Affie's bride. Which came first, Marie Duchess of Edinburgh, which she would become when Affie's wife, or Marie Grand Duchess of Russia? The Liberal Sir Henry Ponsonby, the Queen's private secretary since Lord Grey's death, quoted to his wife the words of Dr Johnson: 'Which comes first, the louse or the flea?' The Queen's feelings of rivalry and jealousy were suddenly exacerbated by news from Germany. The King of Prussia had become Emperor of Germany. The title Empress of India would help to restore the balance.

There was a second personal reason – more romantic and less competitive – for wanting the title. The Queen had always had a special feeling for India and its peoples ever since the country had come under the Crown. She had never travelled there but the Prince of Wales had just made a popular journey. She was a female sovereign and must be allowed to show affection and compassion for her poorest subjects. As time went on, although Queen Victoria was never to visit the Indian subcontinent, she succeeded in creating a Little India at court.

Meanwhile she had entered the most political decade of her life, 1875–1885, under the unique escort of Disraeli. She was to put more and more emphasis on a queen's gifts of humanity and pity, forcing a Vivisection Bill from an uninterested Disraeli, by which the law insisted that experimental research on animals should be humane.

1875 was a great year. Gladstone retired from the leadership of the Liberal Party. With the People's William gone, the People's Victoria felt twice the woman. On the Eastern Question, the Queen wished Disraeli to act with Europe rather than alone with Turkey. The Turkish Sultan, though a Knight of the Garter, was also an alcoholic and was succeeded by his brother, Abdul the Damned. And when the Bulgarian Christians rose against their Turkish masters, incited as the Queen thought by those Russians, Gladstone rose also out of his retirement. Time for the Prime Minister to act!

On 25 November 1875 Dizzy earned his nickname by scaling the heights of financial success. He bought 177,000 of the 400,000 Suez Canal shares; announcing the coup to Queen Victoria he said: 'You have it, Madam . . .' No wonder she told Theodore Martin, Prince Albert's biographer, that Disraeli had '*very lofty views* . . . so much greater than Gladstone's'.[7]

But Gladstone showed that his views, if not lofty, were memorably passionate, by issuing a pamphlet on the Bulgarian atrocities and calling upon the Turkish Bimbashis and Bashibazouks to clear out of poor abused Bulgaria bag and baggage. The Queen was on the rack. Frankly, there was no way of washing her conscience clean of Bashibazouks in the waters of

the Suez Canal. In the end she managed to put the blame on –
those Russians. For it was the Russians who had stirred up the
Bulgarians to rebel against Turkey. She took it as a personal
challenge when Russia declared war on Turkey in 1877, showing
her support for Disraeli's foreign policy by opening Parliament
in February and by lunching with Disraeli at home, Hughenden.
Not for over thirty years had she done such a thing.

At Hughenden, she was pleased to hear that the Turks were
God-fearing, the Bulgarians superstitious and the Russians
perpetrators of the worst possible atrocities. By investing
Turkish hospitals with her 'Order of the Bandage', she was
conferring on them her highest personal award in time of war.
At the same time she kept poor failing Lord Beaconsfield, as
Disraeli now was, up to the mark. Between April 1877 and
February 1878 Queen Victoria suspected a Russian triumph was
being plotted and five times she threatened to abdicate!
Beaconsfield wrote faintly to Lady Bradford of the hyperactive
Faery – now more of an avenging angel. The Queen managed to
encourage the resignation of two of Beaconsfield's more
moderate Ministers, Lord Derby and Lord Carnarvon, the latter
after an extraordinary interview, or rather show-down, with
Majesty. She described Carnarvon afterwards to the Princess
Royal as 'craven-hearted . . . oh! that Englishmen were now
what they were!! but we shall yet assert our rights – & "Britains
never will be Slaves" will yet be our Motto'.[8] The Queen was
appalled at the thought of the Russians getting into Egypt.

The fleet was ordered to Constantinople – then stopped.
Schouvaloff, the Russian Ambassador, expressed the fear that
England was in the control of a mad woman. But Beaconsfield
was in control all right. War and the 'dizzy brink' were avoided
(though Queen Victoria did indulge in a dizzy waltz for the first

time in eighteen years, finding that her son Prince Arthur waltzed just like his beloved father). At last, in June 1878, the movement was definitely away from crisis, with the Congress of Berlin. Beaconsfield described the congress as the surrender of the Emperor of Russia to the Empress of India. Nevertheless, what was later called 'Jingoism' by historians had been born and a popular jingle was chanted in the streets:

We don't want to fight, but by Jingo if we do,
We've got the ships, we've got the men, we've got the money too.

On 16 July 1878 'the old Jew', to quote Bismarck, was the hero of the hour. (*'Der alte Jude, das ist der Mann!'*) Bismarck had given a grand dinner at the congress in Beaconsfield's honour, beginning with champagne and stout, which were followed by dirty stories. Beaconsfield brought back to 10 Downing Street the historic 'Peace with Honour'. Queen Victoria created her Prime Minister a Knight of the Garter. For her, it was the peak of 'high tone' in England. For him it was time for bed – bedtime, he felt, for at least a week.

Queen Victoria had never been working better. There were no more attacks of the dreaded 'nerves' and when a rumour spread that she had committed suicide, she wrote in her journal, 'Quite well'. She was still conscious of her faults, as she always would be, but not all Albert's taboos were still operating. She and her ladies had no hesitation in lighting up a cigarette during the season of midges at Balmoral. As for the taboo on political partisanship, Disraeli had given her confidence in him as well as in herself. Any danger of royal prejudice was avoided by the simple expedient of her being on both sides. Nothing would shake her faith in her own Liberalism.

On the whole her children and grandchildren had now become more of a relaxation than an anxiety. She had the energy to dance reels with her Wales grandsons, Eddy and Georgie (afterwards King George V); her artistic daughter Louise (Loosy) was married to Lord Lorne, now Governor-General of Canada; her favourite son Arthur was engaged to a German princess, Louise Margaret of Prussia (Louischen) who was unhappy at home – typical of the noble young Arthur to rescue her – and incidentally their engagement had taught Queen Victoria quite a lot about the younger generation. As an engaged couple they did not at all mind being stared at, which the Queen described in her journal as 'getting vy American'. Her early instincts to help with a young menage she now perceived to be mistaken, and her new belief was in non-intervention. Princess Alice's family was the only tragic one so far: diphtheria had struck them, killing baby May and striking down Ernie; Alice had given him the kiss of life – Disraeli called it the kiss of death, for Ernie recovered and Alice died on the fatal 14 December 1878, which the Queen called 'most incredible & most mysterious'.[9]

There was also a temperamental change in her attitude to war. She would no longer have approved of John Brown's tendency to pacificism. She strongly endorsed Beaconsfield's militancy, with which, as she told Vicky, she herself had inspired him. The Zulu, Ashanti and Afghan wars were all the necessary concomitant of holding enviable possessions. As she had written to Beaconsfield on 8 July 1879: 'If *we are* to *maintain* our position as a *first-rate* power . . . we must, with our Indian Empire and large Colonies, be *Prepared* for *attacks* and *wars*, *somewhere* or *other*, CONTINUALLY.'[10]

On 3 April 1880 Queen Victoria was abroad, comforted to find that poor darling Alice's room at Darmstadt had been kept exactly as she left it, when what the Queen called 'a terrible telegram' arrived. Lord Beaconsfield's majority had melted away. No doubt to please his Faery, Beaconsfield advised her to send for Lord Hartington. Harty-Tarty, as his friends called him because of his affair with the Duchess of Manchester, refused. He was not quite prime ministerial timber – and Gladstone the Grand Old Man was still around. Gladstone it had to be. On 2 May 1880 Queen Victoria wrote to Vicky that the people's William was 'a most disagreeable person, half crazy'. But the Queen was not Mr Gladstone's worst danger. He was faced with four considerably worse ones: Charles Bradlaugh the Radical atheist MP for Northants; Charles Stewart Parnell and the Irish Home Rulers; Lord Randolph Churchill and what might be called his British Bashibazouks of the Fourth Party; and 'Radical Joe' Chamberlain. Deeply religious, Gladstone would have agreed with Victoria that Bradlaugh was 'horrid' and the worst of the lot. Nevertheless the Queen was a sore trial to the old man (not so grand now) and began by forbidding him to change Beaconsfield's foreign policy in any way.

The Queen did not reject Gladstone's social legislation entirely. The Deceased Wife's Sister (Matrimonial) Bill was thrown out by the bishops; otherwise Princess Beatrice might have suited Alice's widower, Louis. Queen Victoria found that the law as it stood was extremely wasteful of potential royal bridegrooms who happened, sadly, to have been bereaved.

But the Queen had encountered a typical Liberal constitutional problem at the opening of Parliament. When Lord Hartington accidentally forgot to give Queen Victoria the Queen's Speech to read, he said it did not matter, as the so-called Queen's Speech was only the speech of her Ministers. With almost his last breath Lord Beaconsfield contradicted this outrageous heterodoxy. He described Hartington's view as mere parliamentary gossip, thus encouraging the Faery in her quite incorrect opinion of her own ascendancy over her Ministers.

On 19 April 1881 he died at Hughenden. People were surprised that the Queen sent a wreath of primroses, until they read what it said on the card – 'His Favourite Flower'. She believed it was because primroses were wild that he loved them, not because he or they were small or humble. In his memory she set up an enormous tablet above his pew in Hughenden church. After Prince Albert died his widow had felt it was 'still December', well into the next year. Perhaps after Disraeli's death she felt right into the summer that it was 'still April'. For Queen Victoria was in a sense his political widow. Disraeli brought back almost from extinction her natural good spirits and consciousness of vocation. He probably over-emphasised the personal aspect of her constitutional influence, so that she began to think of herself as victorious or defeated as if she were one of her own warriors. She loved the fact that her country getting the Suez Canal was marked with the words, 'You have it, Madam.' She endured the retreat from Kandahar because *she* had made it in response to General Sir Neville Chamberlain's appeal, 'I implore you to come away.'

Meanwhile, Gladstone was predicting the fall of that other grand old institution, the monarchy, as a result of its being pushed too far forward by his late rival. Queen Victoria at this stage of her renaissance was indeed becoming somewhat removed from the ideal constitutional monarch, as depicted by Henry Bagehot, whose triple duty was to advise, to encourage and to warn. Victoria felt it was her duty also to *find out* – particularly what was happening in Gladstone's cabinets. Were there serious dispute? Was the Liberal Government falling apart? Was Lord Hartington, Gladstone's essential aristocratic support, really a Conservative at heart, as Dizzy used to say? Unlike Palmerston and Disraeli himself, Gladstone never told her *everything*.

Gladstone's mission was still to pacify Ireland, but by now the missionary and his mission were about to be swallowed up by the starving natives. The sixty Irish Nationalist MPs who sat in the Parliament at Westminster had a unique leader in the young, white-faced, black-haired Parnell, founder of the Land League to stop rack-renting and a man no less passionate and charismatic than he was alarming. Police reports, on which Queen Victoria relied, gave her no idea of the suffering in Ireland. The compassion she had once shown in response to harrowing stories about Ireland's famine had long since vanished into reliance on coercion and force. She was therefore delighted when Gladstone's Land Bill of July 1880, a typical 'missionary' attempt to end the evictions and murders in Ireland without force, merely resulted in the resignation of a great and good Liberal landlord from Gladstone's cabinet. Lord Lansdowne's resignation was followed by the slaughter of the Land Bill in the House of Lords to the Queen's even greater satisfaction. But this dreadful Bill, as the Queen called it, refused to lie down and die.

Two Radicals in the cabinet, John Bright and Joseph Chamberlain, threatened to resign unless the Land Bill was revived. '*Let* them go' wrote the Queen to Lord Hartington on 12 December 1880.[11] In the same month she was urging W.E. Forster, the Irish Secretary, to resign and was dangling her own abdication in front of his eyes: 'She *cannot* and will *not* be the Queen of a *democratic Monarchy*; and those who have spoken . . . in a very radical sense must look for *another Monarch*; and she doubts they will find one.'[12] Queen Victoria was in no danger of being a democratic monarch; the real point was whether she had behaved as a constitutional one.

With the Queen trying to make the cabinet unworkable, and the Irish MPs succeeding in making the Commons ungovernable, the 'Grand Old Man' was in for a bad time. His reintroduction of a Land Bill in 1881 resulted in the resignation of yet another Liberal grandee from his cabinet. The Duke of Argyll's departure was a blow to the Queen also, for she relied on him – as father-in-law of her daughter Louise – for inside information.

The great nineteenth-century Land Act was finally passed on 22 August 1881 – too late to save Ireland from another burst of violence and 'moonlighting'. In retaliation Parnell was arrested and thrown into Dublin's Kilmainham Gaol; but despite the Queen's exultant telegram to Gladstone – 'Parnell's arrest a great thing' – the resultant chaos could only be tackled by Parnell's release through the negotiations of an inauspicious go-between, Captain O'Shea MP, husband of Parnell's mistress. Things immediately went from bad to worse; much, much worse.

The Irish Secretary, W.E. Forster, deeply resenting the way in which Parnell's release had bypassed his own office, resigned. He was replaced in May 1882 by Lord Frederick Cavendish, husband of Mrs Gladstone's niece Lucy Lyttelton, with Frederick Burke as his under-secretary. While the two Fredericks were crossing Phoenix Park in Dublin to take up their new post, both were murdered. It was 6 May.

Two months earlier, on 2 March 1882, a seventh attempt had been made on the Queen's life. As usual the would-be assassin was a madman rather than a Fenian. The Queen's carriage was standing at Windsor station when Roderick McLean fired. Two Eton boys beat him off with their umbrellas while Brown protected Her Majesty. Queen Victoria felt that the attack was almost worth it, as it brought out the people's intense loyalty. Next month – on 27 April 1882 – their loyalty was boosted by that ever-popular event, a royal marriage. The stricken Prince Leopold happily married Princess Helen of Waldeck. The Queen celebrated by wearing white over her black dress for the first time since Albert's death – it was her own white wedding veil. Leopold had already been granted his wish to be created a royal duke (Albany) on condition that he remained Prince Leopold in the Queen's house. For, as the Queen whimsically observed: 'no one can be a Prince, but anyone can be a duke.'[13] Ten months after his marriage Leopold, shortest lived of all the Queen's children, was to father a daughter, Princess Alice, who would live to be ninety-eight, the longest lived of all Queen Victoria's grandchildren.

As the family moved into 1883 the Queen felt herself getting stronger and busier while Gladstone became weaker and more and more unequal to his task. This seemed to her the right way round. In one drawing-room he did not even hear what she said to him. 'The Diplomatic Corps are numerous to-day,' she remarked, to which he replied, thinking she had said something about the Siamese suite who were passing, 'Yes, they are very ugly.'[14]

On Easter Sunday, 1883, the Queen received news that John Brown was ill in the Clarence Tower, Windsor. She too was ill, with rheumatism after a fall. Jenner and Dr Reid nursed both of them. The Queen slowly recovered. Brown died on 29 March, it was said of a chill contracted while hunting for Fenians in the bushes, or of erysipelas, or of the bottle. Queen Victoria said of Brown to the Crathie minister, 'He became my best & truest friend – as I was his.' She compared the shock of Brown's death to one of those shocks that had struck in 1861. Note that she did not refer to THE shock – Albert's death – but 'one of those', perhaps the death of her mother or one of the Coburg princes. With the combination of shock and rheumatism, she could neither walk nor even stand till June. She needed a masseuse – first a Madame Nautet, then a Mrs Cash, recommended by the writer John Ruskin. But most of all she needed John Brown's strong arm to give her support.

Queen Victoria was approaching the summit of the Brown saga. She commissioned the sculptor Edgar Boehm to execute a statue in Brown's memory; the Poet Laureate, Lord Tennyson, was responsible for two very lame lines of verse:

> Friend more than servant, loyal, truthful, brave:
> Self less than duty even to the grave.

To match the statue at Balmoral was a granite seat at Osborne in Brown's memory.

The summit of the saga, a sad one, was reached when Queen Victoria asked Sir Theodore Martin, Prince Albert's official biographer, to write the *Life* of John Brown from his diaries. Martin declined on the grounds of his wife Lady Martin's ill-health. The assignment was perhaps given to a woman journalist; whatever the case, Ponsonby saw a suspicious Miss MacGregor hanging around at Osborne.

The Queen was working on her own second volume of *Leaves*: entitled *More Leaves from the Journals of our Life in The Highlands*, it was dedicated to the late John Brown and published in 1884. Nearly everybody liked it for one reason or another: the Court because it gave Her Majesty so much pleasure and Max Beerbohm, thirty-five years later, as a perfect subject for parody. As usual only her own family was critical, the Prince of

Wales complaining that his name did not appear in it once. Five times, was his mother's retort.

This was not all that the Queen was working on. After all, was she not an author? Had not Disraeli himself told her so? ('We authors, Ma'am'.) So on 23 February 1884 Ponsonby received a manuscript from Queen Victoria which she told him was the first draft of a memoir of John Brown. Miss MacGregor was correcting it for repetitions, but she still needed help. And her object? To show her gratitude to Brown and to prove that he was not just a devoted servant but 'a great deal more'.[15] Despite Victoria's having stated it was for private circulation only, Ponsonby bravely said he thought the possible unfavourable criticism by strangers of the Queen's most sacred feelings would cause Her Majesty pain. The Queen understandably replied by thanking Sir Henry but reminding him that the memoir was not for publication. Neither of them went into what John Brown *was* if he was more than a devoted servant. A second royal note asked for the manuscript back to show it to Lord Rowton, Disraeli's former secretary. Ponsonby saw Rowton after the latter had read the text. Delay at all costs, was Rowton's advice. Let a single confidential man print Brown's diary. This would take six months, by which time HM would have seen how impossible it was.

Rowton's little plot to delay everything must have failed, for on 16 March the situation deteriorated: Randall Davidson, the courageous Dean of Windsor, gave HM a broad hint, while thanking her for his copy of her *More Leaves*, that there must not be *More Leaves Still*; Victoria haughtily announced that more still were indeed planned. The Dean objected again in writing; HM ordered him to withdraw and apologise for the pain caused; the Dean apologised without withdrawing and – silence. Victoria spoke not a word to the Dean, and on Sunday another occupied his pulpit. Then, suddenly, it was all over. A smiling Queen Victoria sent for Dean Davidson. The memoir was never mentioned again. And Arthur Ponsonby, Sir Henry's son and biographer, stated that his father destroyed the Brown memoir.

That was all very well, but the twentieth century was to have its own Brown legends. Lionel Logue, the eminent speech therapist who worked successfully on George VI's stammer, was said to have told his spiritualist friends, such as Hannen Swaffer, that he had actually seen the Brown memoir closely guarded in a royal cupboard. The evidence for this legend is nil, and Logue's family do not believe it. Nor does that particular legend reveal what the Queen wrote about Brown in the hidden memoir. But another typical myth of an even later date was launched by the writer E.E.P. Tisdall, who described how a love-note from Queen Victoria to John Brown mysteriously came into his possession. As it vanished again, equally mysteriously, its authenticity cannot now be assessed. There are in fact at least four objects, counting the love-note as one, that belong to the legendary or uninvestigated aspect of Victoria's reign and all have mysteriously vanished, possibly into the mists of human imagination: Prince Albert's document of 1861 alleged to have been briefly 'discovered' by a researcher (or hoaxer) in the Windsor Archives wherein the Prince notified his intention to the Privy Council of seeking a divorce; John Brown's gold watch, supposedly presented to him by the Queen for spiritualist achievements and stolen from the Psychological Society in the 1960s; and John Brown's hidden diary and memoir, allegedly hidden rather than destroyed but certainly vanished.

Perhaps the safest comment on all these 'disappearances' is that they reflect the mixture of surprise and disbelief that Queen Victoria's life came to arouse. They fired the public imagination, and no wonder. Nevertheless one letter that the Queen wrote after Brown's death shows clearly that he was no more than a friend, though a very close one. It was sent to her grandson Prince George of Wales, the future King George V. 'I have lost my *dearest best* friend', she wrote, 'who no one in this world can ever replace . . . never forget your poor sorrowing old Grandmama's *best & truest* friend . . .'[16] It is unthinkable that a woman like Queen Victoria should have picked out the young Prince for her guilty confidences if she had indeed been having a sexual affair with the 'friend'.

But she never deviated from the word 'friend' – and it was a two-way word, as in the simple hand-written message she sent on Brown's elaborate printed card on New Year's Day 1877:

> To my best friend J.B.
> From his best friend VRI.

The strange story of Queen Victoria and John Brown culminated in the claims of a man living in Paris who said he was their son.

But stranger still is the most recent story according to which Victoria's eldest son was born to her at the age of fifteen and raised abroad, his father being the 1st Duke of Wellington, then aged sixty-five. The claims made by a Portuguese writer, as this book went to the printers, that such a son existed, and that he, the writer, is descended from the son, cannot be admitted. Wellington was not a baby-snatcher and Victoria, as a girl, slept in her mother's bedroom, spending the days guarded by her governess Baroness Lehzen. At least three other families claim descent from Wellington because of a 'nasal' resemblance. This will not do as evidence.

Poor rebellious Prince Leopold certainly was her child, although by no means her favourite, and she honoured him deeply when he died the year after Brown from a brain haemorrhage. She realised, however, that they must not 'repine', for he always was, and always would be, consumed with a 'restless longing' for what he could never have – 'namely, a normal life'.[17]

It is possible to wonder whether a woman as clear-eyed as the Queen often was, ever applied these thoughts to her other children, especially the younger ones. Did she ever feel that some of the restrictions on the royal family were out of date in the 1880s? There was Princess Louise battling to become an artist and Princess Beatrice not allowed to battle for a husband against Mama's prior claim on her services. Was Leo the only one to fight against 'restless longings'? And what of Majesty herself?

Unfortunately almost all the Queen's 'restless longings' were concentrated on getting rid of Gladstone, though his government did set up a Royal Commission on Housing. (The Prince of Wales sat on it when not otherwise engaged.) But nothing could eliminate the Queen's painful, deep-seated jealousy of Gladstone and when, in an excess of 'weariness', he joined a VIP trip to Copenhagen, where he hobnobbed with the Emperor of Russia without her permission or foreknowledge, she wrote him off for good. If he was so 'weary', why not resign?

When Ponsonby and the Queen at last received the good news – from Gladstone himself – that he would retire after the summer of 1885, they believed it. No one reckoned on a Home Rule crisis. Gladstone could retire from anything but his mission to Ireland. But even before Home Rule tore Gladstone and the British cabinet to pieces, the Grand Old Man was challenged elsewhere in a way that set him directly against Queen Victoria.

The defeat of the nationalist leader Arabi at Tel-el-kebir in Egypt had not brought peace. Revolt flared up in the Sudan under a fakir calling himself the Mahdi, the Expected One. The Queen had not expected any such person, but now, expecting the worst results for the safety of Suez and India, she repeatedly encouraged Gladstone to halt the Mahdi forthwith. The last month of 1883 had opened with a disaster. On 3 December a strong force of Egyptians under Hicks Pasha was wiped out by the Mahdi. But instead of New Year 1884 opening with counter operations, the Queen's journal was full of the government doing 'nothing' and herself telegraphing and writing to them 'continually'.

Suddenly, when the Prime Minister was indisposed, his cabinet acted – and did far too much. They sent out General Gordon, a specialist in victory not in evacuation, to rescue the Mahdi's potential victims and retreat with them to safety. Charles George Gordon, a mystic of fifty-one who carried a Bible and a cane into battle, was the brilliantly wrong man for the job. He felt his duty was the Mahdi's defeat not his own retreat. This meant waiting in Khartoum for the reinforcements that never came – not while Gordon was still alive. But from 18 February 1884, when Gordon had arrived in Khartoum, officially to wind up British rule in the Sudan, he waited. On 14 December, which was of course to Queen Victoria the most fatal day of the whole year, Gordon wrote the last entry in his Khartoum diary: 'Now mark THIS, if the expedition does not come in ten days The Town May Fall; and I have done my best for the honour of our country. Goodbye. C.G. Gordon . . .' On 26 January 1885 the siege ended with the Mahdi's men bursting into the palace and spearing the hero to death. Two days later the first reinforcements arrived. A week later still, the Queen deliberately forgot her constitutional duty to 'advise' and 'warn'. Instead she used Gordon's death as a means of publicly exposing Gladstone for the disaster she felt he was. She telegraphed to him e*n clair* so that all the world might learn her view: 'These news from Khartoum are frightful, and to think that all this might have been prevented . . . is too frightful.'[18]

From the point of view of history's judgment of Queen Victoria, her emotional behaviour was doubly regrettable. For during the year 1884 while Gordon was besieged in the Sudan, she had shown that she could work remarkably well with Gladstone for the good of the country and of posterity. The Liberals had promised to introduce a third Reform Bill in 1884, so that the vote might be extended from the boroughs to the counties. Having passed the Commons, their Bill was thrown out by the Tory House of Lords under its leader, the Marquess of Salisbury. But Salisbury saw a way out. If the new Reform Bill were also to include a redistribution of seats, this would save the Tories from being swamped by the new voters. The Queen appointed herself intermediary between Lords and Commons, inspired by two thoughts. First, the respectable working class deserved the vote. Second, the danger was that an obdurate House of Lords would be brought down by Mr Gladstone's radical 'wild men', who would in turn attack all authority including the monarchy. They were already chanting slogans against the Lords: 'Peers v. People', 'Ancient Monuments', 'Interesting Ruins' . . . With effective seriousness the Queen warned Lord Salisbury against opposing the *principle* of Reform. And so with the Queen's genuine help, Gladstone's Third Reform Bill reached the statute book just before the personal relationship of this redoubtable pair went up in flames.

A surprising result emerged from the political manoeuvres before the autumn election of 1885. Parnell ordered all the Irish to vote Conservative after a secret pact with Lord Carnarvon, the Tory Irish Viceroy. Gladstone left the Radicals under Chamberlain to make the running on the home front, though he stood again himself at the election instead of retiring as promised.

In the event, Lord Salisbury found himself able to form a government, provided he had the support of Irish MPs, while Gladstone came out for Home Rule, the policy of those Irish MPs. There was political turmoil. The Queen worked frantically between settling in a new dogs' home and furthering her favourite concept of a Liberal coalition, which in fact amounted to moderate Conservatism. In high hopes, she opened Parliament on 21 January 1886, lame though she was; but the Salisbury government was fatally weakened by the Viceroy's resignation over coercion. For the first time a minister dared to tell the Queen that the Irish felt no loyalty to her personally, being concerned solely with independence. It was the last time that Victoria was to open Parliament in person.

Five days later the Liberals and Parnell combined to defeat Salisbury. The Queen's reaction to this blow shows that she did not yet quite understand the working of the parliamentary system and the monarchy's place in it. After failing to persuade Lord Salisbury to withdraw his resignation, she sent for Gladstone by word of mouth on 29 January in the hope that her verbal message could be cancelled at the last moment. Poor old Gladdy, as Ponsonby called him, was touched by HM's personal message, not realising its significance.

At his first audience the unhappy new Prime Minister was informed by the Queen that foreign policy must *not* be changed, nor must 'rosewater' Granville become Foreign Secretary. Gladstone wrung his hands; he might have been tempted to wring the Queen's neck had he realised that these illiberal terms had been drawn up by HM in collusion with the defeated Tory Prime Minister. She did not mind anyone knowing that to her Gladstone was merely 'this half crazy and in many ways really ridiculous old man'.[19] The fact that crazy or popular, old or grand, Gladstone was still her First Minister pricked her conscience not at all.

Lord Salisbury gave her another piece of daringly partisan advice: to consult the Tory ex-Minister Lord Goschen just as she had consulted the retired Duke of Wellington in the past. (But Goschen was an active politician, not retired into elder-statesmanship like the great Duke.) Salisbury also gave some not very constitutional advice to Lord Rosebery, the new Liberal Foreign Secretary: that he should deal direct with HM and the PM, bypassing as far as possible the Liberal cabinet. It may be that the Queen's success in smoothing the path of the Third Reform Bill went to her head, leaving her with the fatal impression that moderate bi-partisanship, in which she rightly believed, was the same thing as plain bias, which she repudiated but nevertheless practised. Perhaps the worst example of bias occurred throughout March and April 1886, when Queen Victoria was sending Lord Salisbury copies of Gladstone's letters to her. Happily, Salisbury's comments on them were moderate and innocuous.

The great Home Rule explosion put an end to all fine distinctions – and tore up the last shreds of royal neutrality. In March 1886 it was Gladstone and Parnell against the world. Gladstone's right-hand man, Lord Hartington, had refused to join a cabinet devoted to Home Rule. More surprisingly, the great Radical, Joseph Chamberlain, had tried to satisfy the Irish Nationalists with a bill for local self-government instead of full-fledged Home Rule. The wild men promised to dump him in a bog-hole if he visited Ireland. Finally, when Chamberlain learned that Gladstone's bill did not envisage any more Irish MPs at Westminster (thought to keep a brake on the wild men), Chamberlain and G.M. Trevelyan, a distinguished Liberal, resigned. Let them go, thought Gladstone, just as Queen Victoria had viewed the Radicals earlier.

Despite the Liberal split, Gladstone introduced his Home Rule Bill on 8 April 1886, involving Irish land reform as well as self-government. He spoke for three hours and twenty minutes. When he finally fell into bed exhausted, his wife kept all messages till morning, merely tying knots in his night gown. Next morning the PM was all tied up in knots. This was true of his political prospects also. For on 15 April there was a vast anti-Home Rule meeting of united Tories and Liberals, including Salisbury and Hartington in the Opera House. The Queen was transported, though she would have liked to hear more still from Salisbury; perhaps even a touch of that 'stump' oratory she had found so undignified in Gladstone.

But neither Salisbury nor Gladstone was capable of doing all she wanted done, especially in foreign affairs. For example, there was beloved Sandro (Prince Alexander of Battenburg) who had lost his Bulgarian throne through those Russian 'fiends', and no one could put him back.

An event was looming that would persuade Queen Victoria to rely only on herself in the greatest matters.

SEVEN

JUBILEES GOLDEN, DIAMOND AND WHITE, 1887–1901

The great event already looming on the horizon was, of course, the Queen's golden jubilee. On 20 June 1887 she would be 'Fifty Years a Queen', as the papers never stopped saying. It had been preceded by the defeat of Gladstone's great Home Rule Bill, thanks to the withdrawal of his radical and Whig support and – it must be admitted – to the Queen's own hard work. She threw her weight against Gladstone and on to the side of Salisbury. Exhausted as she was, she said, by having worked harder in the previous twenty-four years than ever before in her life, she decided to take her summer holiday in far-away Balmoral instead of accessible Osborne, so as not to become 'a Slave of the H[ouse] of C[ommons] & of the GOM.'[1]

Looked at the other way round, it was not slavery to support her Prime Minister of the day, but her constitutional duty, as she was always explaining to her foreign relatives. Nevertheless, she sincerely thought it was for the overriding good of the country that she should encourage the opposition to Irish Home Rule.

The Queen was determined from the start that her jubilee should show the other side of her nature: Victoria the mother. She even begged Lord Salisbury, during the election campaign that followed Gladstone's defeat in Parliament, to treat the Irish as gently as possible. The whole scene and tone of the jubilee were set by Victoria's own dress. Away with spikey, sparkling crowns! Bonnets would be worn. (The Victorian bonnet was an essentially feminine attribute. After the Queen was dead, an old fisherman in the South of France remembered her for her enjoyment of their *bouillabaisse* soup and her magnificent purple bonnet.)

Of course the Queen's children were horrified by the idea of a regal bonnet instead of a crown and sent in Princess Alexandra of Wales – their mother's favourite – to put the case for the crown. The Princess came tumbling out of the Queen's room, quaking. She had never been so snubbed. As a literary critic once put it: 'She ruled her people like a mother and her family like a queen.'

Queen Victoria's case for the bonnet was based on her jubilee status as mother, grandmother and great-grandmother, rather than as ruler. To her, there was no danger of a Queen-Empress losing her authority by emphasising her motherhood. With her children she was always a parent, not a companion, or confidante, or 'best friend', as some modern theorists might prefer. And parent ultimately meant the commanding voice, the last say, the authority.

Queen Victoria's active motherliness was reserved above all for those developing races who had captured her imagination. Through her children's marriages she had become Grandmother of Europe; through her own imaginative sympathies she had become mother of her far-flung peoples, especially the Indians.

Meanwhile, on Jubilee Day 1887 she wore herself to a shred with celebrations, original and traditional. Her journal opened as was right and proper with a celebration of Albert: '. . . I am alone, though surrounded by many dear children . . . fifty years ago today since I came to the Throne! God has supported me through many great trials and sorrows.'[2]

There was breakfast at Windsor under the Frogmore trees, followed by a drive through cheering crowds to Windsor station; the train journey to London, more cheering crowds on the way to the Palace; and a luncheon table glittering with orchids and exotic royalties. In the evening there was another huge meal, a 'family dinner' for over fifty Royal and Serene Highnesses – one for each year of her reign with a few to spare – all eating off gold plate. On her right sat the King of Denmark, on her left the King of Greece, and opposite, the King of the Belgians. At last the long 'family day' was over and she slipped away for one more task that still remained: to write up her journal, a duty that could never, never be shirked.

The thanksgiving service was held next day at Westminster Abbey. There was no crown or robes of state, of course; much less the glass coach. But she did allow six of the famous cream horses to draw her open landau and, more importantly, she ordered an escort of Indian cavalry, a significant aspect of the jubilee, which had already brought the Queen closer to her Empire with the opening of the Imperial Institute in London. When she requested a leper colony to celebrate with an increased ration of rice, they telegraphed her their best wishes for a reign of 10,000 years.

Through the long summer she was frequently 'dissolved' by heat and exhaustion. There was the children's party in Hyde Park, where a small girl spotted a large balloon rising from the grass and shouted, 'There's Queen Victoria going to Heaven!' The Royal Society for the Prevention of Cruelty to Animals and the Battersea Dogs' Home both celebrated in the most august of all temples – the Albert Hall. Osborne was her base for attending the mighty Spithead naval review, and at last, after a record of hundreds of events and thousands of telegrams read, she faded away to Balmoral, to recover and take stock.

Golden jubilee year, 1887, had left Queen Victoria with two consuming interests, one tragic, the other self-fulfilling. Her eldest daughter Vicky was about to become German Empress through the imminent succession of her husband Fritz to the Imperial throne. Queen Victoria had noted that in the golden jubilee procession of 21 June 'dear Fritz' had outshone all the rest, with his golden beard and helmet and snowy white uniform – a Charlemagne among ordinary mortals. But it was Fritz who was mortal; he was dying of throat cancer, though the Queen's misguided doctor, Morell Mackenzie, had persuaded Fritz that the cancer had been cured without an operation. Sure enough, Fritz's cancer returned in the November of jubilee year and he ascended the Imperial throne on 9 March 1888, to reign for ninety-nine days only. 'My OWN dear Empress Victoria,' wrote the Queen to her daughter on 16 March, with a brave attempt at triumph, and on 22 April the dauntless old lady was paying a private farewell visit to Fritz in Berlin, which included meeting Chancellor Bismarck himself. After the dying Emperor's mother-in-law had come and gone, Bismarck mopped his brow and said, 'That was a woman! One could do business with her!'

The Emperor Frederick died on 15 June 1888. Queen Victoria's letter to her tragic daughter had a very different beginning from the one of March: 'My Darling, darling unhappy Child . . .' It was to be Vicky's own eldest child, now Kaiser William II, who would cause much of that unhappiness.

The second, more exhilarating idea associated with jubilee year was Queen Victoria's love affair with the colonial races. This should long ago have become one of the hallmarks of her greatness, but it was scarcely mentioned by historians before the Second World War. It was only after the disintegration of European colonial empires, Britain's included, that racism became a dirty word. Then, for the first time, it was realised that the Great White Queen held a special brief for her brown and black peoples, and that Queen Victoria could lecture reactionary courtiers on the evils of racial prejudice every bit as eloquently as any member of an international movement today.

At the golden jubilee of 1887 even Liberal Sir Henry Ponsonby was puzzled by the fuss that 'they' were making of the Indians on the Day. Why an *Indian* escort for the Queen-Empress? The fact was that Queen Victoria's own predelictions had combined with world measures of improvement to bring forward her Indians. It was a pleasure to be served by Indians; it was her duty to encourage the education and development of these fascinating people. She made no distinction in her mind between Muslims and Hindus, though all her servants were Muslims from Agra. This provided its own complications. Mahomet was sleek and smiling, Abdul Karim slim, clever and twenty-four. The Queen's creative imagination, dormant since John Brown's death, sprang to excited life, envisaging a new, cultured Karim who would have an English tutor, would serve the Queen exclusively, just as Brown had, and finally would teach an equally aspiring Queen to speak a few words of Hindustani. Why not? She was informed that Abdul's father was a doctor in Agra, surely one of India's social leaders. (Actually, Abdul's father simply worked as a chemist in Agra gaol as the anti-Indian officials were quick to discover.)

There were only four years between the death of the Queen's first exotic servant, her Highland attendant, in 1883, and the rise of her second exotic servant, her Indian attendant, in 1887; and in some sense Abdul Karim was clearly a reincarnation of John Brown. But whereas the Queen had to defend Brown only within the intimate circle of her family and Court, with Karim she felt it her duty to put his case to the India Office, Foreign Office, Prime Minister and even Viceroy of the day. At sixty-eight, she was as effective a fighter for the Indians as she had been at forty-six when it first seemed her duty to stand up for Brown – 'poor good Brown'.

The first racial prejudice showed itself when the Queen decided to recuperate at Cimiez after the ordeal of the golden jubilee. Abdul Karim was already on the way up. As her Indian teacher, a 'Munshi', he protested against photographs of himself waiting at table, and the Queen ordered all menial pictures to be destroyed. When she had him painted by the great Joachim von Angeli, no less, it was against a background of gold rather than a backdrop of kitchens. Now she decided to take him with her to the South of France. But her staff refused to have him in their carriage or at their table. On hearing this, HM swept everything off the top of her dressing-table on to the floor. It was one of her now rare rages.

The Queen had no doubt been lacking in tact, but it was Karim who made the next mistake, a mistake that was to threaten his whole career. Without the Queen's permission, he invited an Indian friend, Ahmed Raffiudin, into the royal villa and entertained him there. Ahmed was a respectable journalist writing on the *Nineteenth Century* magazine. Officialdom immediately equated 'journalist' with 'spy' and pictured Ahmed and Abdul extracting secrets from the Queen's state boxes, for transmission to the politically active Muslims of Agra.

It was all a nonsense. After long, painful exchanges of letters between Queen and Ministers, it was at last established that the

Munshi's pretensions and his security risks were both equally unreal. A sympathetic Lord Salisbury left behind a fascinating correspondence with the Queen on the subject among his papers at Christ Church, Oxford. They do him credit.

Queen Victoria too did herself credit. In certain perverse moods she would protest that she would rather abdicate and emigrate to Australia than be a 'democratic Monarch'. Yet her outspoken attacks on racial prejudice were sincere, valuable and unique. The Empress of India had indeed justified herself and pushed history another step along the road to true humanity. A favourite quotation of hers for use against reactionary courtiers went as follows: (Queen Victoria is writing to Lord Salisbury in the third person. on 11 March 1898, about the Munshi's social position) 'It is *not* a high one & it is *not* in *England* that *one* should speak of *that* . . .'[3] She would then go on to remind her questioner of the famous butcher who sired an Archbishop – they could do such things in England – and her questioner would realise she was asking why, if an Archbishop's father could be a butcher, a Munshi's father could not be a chemist? (It is sad to have to record that King Edward VII, after his mother's death in 1901, had all the Munshi's papers burnt. However, Edward's natural kindliness reasserted itself after the Munshi died at Karim Lodge in 1909. The King granted Mrs Karim's request to keep a few of Queen Victoria's letters written to the Munshi in her own hand.)

Between the two jubilees, golden and diamond, it was Bertie, Prince of Wales, and William, German Emperor, who presented Queen Victoria with some of her worst moments.

Bertie was again in court, under a subpoena, over the Tranby Croft gambling case of 1891, to be known as the Baccarat case. Though Bertie was innocent, it was again felt that the heir to the throne was keeping the wrong company. His host Gordon

Cumming was the cheat – and a witty foreign cartoon retranslated the Prince of Wales's motto, *Ich Dien* ('I serve'), as *Ich Deal*.

Kaiser William sacrificed his beloved Grandmama's esteem, which meant much to him, for the pleasure of insulting England over the disastrous Jameson Raid. A fatal burst of patriotic imperialism persuaded Dr Jameson and his friends, almost certainly in collusion with Joseph Chamberlain the Colonial Secretary, to rise against President Kruger's Boer Republic and declare for Britain. Unsupported, the raiders were all rounded up and captured in the early days of 1896. It was a sorry prologue to the Queen's Diamond Jubilee of 1897, made worse by the telegram of congratulation sent to Kruger by the young Kaiser. Worse still, the raid turned out to be the direct cause of the Boer or South African War. The conflict ensured that a long shadow would fall across Queen Victoria's last years.

But at least the hostilities gave the Queen, always conscious of being a soldier's daughter, the chance to steady those suffering from doubts with one of her memorable sayings. During the Black Week of the war, Queen Victoria was visited at Windsor by Arthur Balfour, a future Conservative Prime Minister. Balfour's philosophical features never exactly radiated confidence about anything and perhaps Black Week made him look particularly lugubrious and doubtful. The Queen was having none of it. Her sight was failing and it was bad enough having to cope with these dark December days. 'Please understand,' she said, 'that there is no one depressed in this house; we are not interested in the possibilities of defeat; they do not exist.'[4] By the Queen's last years, when her country's imperialism had already passed its peak, she had worked out a rule-of-thumb political philosophy for herself: Britain should not try to grab more lands – but to lose what we had once held was always bad.

Queen Victoria would have felt herself lucky to spend all her last years entirely in the hands of Conservative governments. The Liberals, however, did make one comeback between her two jubilees, with the incomparable Mr Gladstone still at their head. The Queen and Gladstone had played hide-and-seek with each other during the golden jubilee garden party, the old man trying for a *tête-à-tête*, the old lady always giving him the slip. But Gladstone was back for the fourth and positively last time as PM in 1892. At his first audience the Queen noticed a weird look in his eyes. He may have noticed the same thing in hers. Those protuberant blue eyes were seldom able to hide the jealousy and animosity in her soul. By 1892 she was describing Gladstone as 'a poor but wicked' old man, more than half crazy.

But as usual, worse than the GOM himself were many of the dangerous men who fought under his colours. Henry Labouchère, for instance, the notorious atheist who suggested that Buckingham Palace should be used as a home for fallen women. More dangerous still was the Irish MP and leader of the Home Rulers, Charles Stewart Parnell. When Captain William O'Shea MP, husband of Parnell's mistress, Kitty, divorced his wife, the effect was to divorce Gladstone from the Parnellites. Home Rule was defeated by the House of Lords in 1893, a portrait of the ignoble scene being hung later in a corridor leading to the Lords' library. Parnell died in 1895 and Gladstone resigned for the last time, in 1894, as Liberal leader.

Gladstone would not perhaps have said that nothing became Queen Victoria in her life like her attitude to his leaving office. He compared her parting from him to his own parting from the mule that had served him long and faithfully on a Sicilian holiday. Though grateful, he could neither like the brute nor regret it. Victoria was more likely to love the mule than to like

Gladstone, for the mule was a dumb animal, and Gladstone talked so much. As things were, she always conceded that Gladstone was a good man, despite the malicious rumours about his rescue work with fallen women in the streets of London.

* * *

Death had struck much of the sparkle from the opening of golden jubilee year. On 16 January 1887, Princess Beatrice heard that her husband, Prince Henry of Battenburg, was suffering from slight fever contracted at the Ashanti War. A white-faced Prince Arthur brought in the fatal telegram on the 22nd to say that beloved Liko was dead. For once the Queen could hardly express her feelings, even in her journal. Liko had been 'the sunshine in the home', and she seemed to be back in the dreadful time after Albert's and Leopold's deaths, rather than three weeks into jubilee year.

If Liko was the light of the home, their home had ceased to be his light. He felt stifled by the eternal round of Balmoral, Osborne and Windsor, and may have been partially consoling himself with unhappily married, childless Princess Louise. At least Beatrice was the mother of four children.

The other family death that blighted the early1890s may have turned out to be a gift of God to all concerned, though no one would have dared to say so. The Prince of Wales's eldest son and heir, Albert Victor (Eddy), a somewhat disappointing character though not unattractive to women, was due to marry Princess May of Teck on 27 February 1891. On 9 January a telegram arrived from Sandringham to say that he had influenza. It turned to pneumonia and on 14 January he was dead. On 13 March of this same bad year, 1891, the Queen heard that Louis, Grand Duke of Hesse, Alice's husband, had also died. The Queen felt she could scarcely bear yet another sorrow but remembered in time that her new motto was 'Still Endure' – those words spoken to her by a mysterious voice after Albert's death. She had been able to tell Vicky about the voice and message after Fritz's death four years previously. And indeed it turned out to be the right motto, for in due course Princess May married the admirable Georgie, Bertie's eldest surviving son. Georgie, who was to become King George V, was found by his delighted Grandmama to be still interested in the last relics of Victorian magic – 'improvement'. He intended to improve himself. On 14 December 1895, Georgie's second son was born. Queen Victoria's attendants trembled to think what she would make of the terrible date, but she said that the child might be a gift of God. He became King George VI, father of Queen Elizabeth II.

Queen Victoria wrote in her journal with a forgiveable flourish on 23 September 1896: 'Today is the day on which I have reigned longer, by a day, than any English sovereign.'[5] Of course the diamond jubilee began, like all junketings, with headaches. How to cram kings, emperors and their suites into Windsor Castle and Buckingham Palace? At the Queen's age it was almost enough to turn her against the whole thing.

Questions of precedence she found merely troublesome, rather than of deeply royal import. Though her daughter Lenchen came to her assistance in drawing up the processions through London's streets, they were always forgetting some prince or other and then arguing about his rank and style. On one point the Queen was adamant. No Kaiser – or no procession. Kaiser William II was wildly unpopular with her people because of his violent words during a quarrel between Turkey and Greece; she dared not let him parade himself. So her young Private Secretary, Arthur Bigge, had the not unpleasant task of relaying Her Majesty's words to the Prince of Wales: '. . . there is not the slightest fear of the Queen giving way over Kaiser William's coming here in June. It would never do.'[6]

It was virtually Queen Victoria herself who chose the national name for her great commemoration – the Diamond Jubilee, turning down undesirables such as Jubilissime and Queen's Year. The actual anniversary fell on 20 June, a Sunday, so the great day began for the Queen with a family service in St George's Chapel followed by a quiet visit by her and Vicky to Albert's Mausoleum at Frogmore. Albert's T*e Deum* was sung in all churches, chapels and synagogues throughout the land at their own thanksgiving services.

Queen Victoria then drove through London in her carriage drawn by eight cream horses, pausing for the briefest possible thanksgiving service on the steps of St Paul's Cathedral. A full-scale, hot service in Westminster Abbey would have been beyond her strength. True, one suggestion had been to manhandle the carriage up the steps and into the cathedral; another suggestion from a well-wisher was to replace HM temporarily by a puppet Queen, to save unnecessary exertion. Fortunately Victoria's German relatives did not hear of these ideas, for even the outdoor service was enough to shock Augusta Strelitz. 'No!' she gasped, 'after 60 years Reign, to thank God in the Street!' A brave attempt to exploit the new techniques of cinematography had an unexpected result: it looked as though the Queen was thanking God in a blizzard.

No critical spirit such as Augusta's invaded the press. Ecstatic articles celebrated Queen Victoria's 'Sixty Glorious Years' – the length and splendour of her reign. Only *The Times* seemed to be maintaining a sense of proportion in an article on 'The World's

Longest Reigns' – until *The Times* revealed that, according to his country's tradition, King Feridoon of Persia had been on his throne for 500 years!

The golden jubilee had failed to produce a golden aftermath; indeed one of the years that the Queen called 'horrid' – 1892 – came exactly between the two jubilees, landing her with the defeat of Salisbury and the return of Gladstone. She never understood her country's party system, being aghast that a minister as efficient as Lord Salisbury should be at the mercy of mere voters. No one asked her who, under her reformed party system, would judge the suitability of ministers. Perhaps herself? The mere voters, however, gave Salisbury a crushing victory in 1895, big enough to see out even the immortal Queen.

In the year following the diamond jubilee came a death that did not have to be faced stoically by the Queen – that of Gladstone. There was no need to say 'Still endure' when the GOM died on 19 May, for he had already lost his power to hurt her. In praising his good points after his death, she revealed, perhaps unconsciously, what it was that made him unendurable to her. 'He had a wonderful power of speaking,' she wrote in her journal, 'and carrying the masses with him.' With the People's William out of the way at last, the People's Victoria could afford to be kind to Mrs Gladstone, whom she genuinely liked; though it was vexing that Bertie should be one of the GOM's pall-bearers. Her courtiers may not have told her that Gladstone's wish for the diamond jubilee had been Queen Victoria's abdication in favour of her heir.

The death of her cousin Mary, Duchess of Teck, in 1898 inspired Queen Victoria to draw up plans for her own funeral: no black mourning, a proper embalmment and the coffin crammed with the photographs and mementos of loved ones – a veritable Pandora's box of treasures, with beloved Albert's padded dressing-gown in pride of place and good John Brown's photograph on her wrist. The Munshi and Sahl, her German librarian, were both to march in the procession.

The second of Victoria's 'horrid' years was 1900, preceded as it was by the outbreak of the Boer War. The conflict, however, gave the old Queen the chance to contemplate one of her favourite duties – distributing medals. She was also able to fight for a granddaughter in trouble. Marie-Louise of Schleswig-Holstein (Louie) had taken refuge from her cruel husband, Prince Aribert of Anhalt, in Canada. Now Louie was summoned by Aribert to face divorce in Germany. Victoria's authentic voice sounded in the message she sent to Canada's Governor-General: 'Tell my granddaughter to come home to me. VRI.'

* * *

Queen Victoria crossed the sea for the last time in April 1900 when she paid an inspired visit to Ireland. She said it was entirely her own idea and she did her royal best to make it seem a good one. The fact was that the war against the Boers had made her unpopular in France. Her usual visit to Cimiez was deemed unwise and even Italy might prove a risk. So she gave up the 'flowery South' altogether and spent three weeks of spring touring Ireland.

Why was rebellious Ireland thought to be safer than the Continent? Fritz Ponsonby, on her staff, could hear what he called the 'bagpipe drone' of booing at the back of the cheering crowds. Luckily she was too deaf by now to hear anything but the loyalists' patriotic screams. There were few flags in Dublin's back streets and the police arrested those who tore down the decorations. Round and round Phoenix Park she rode in a donkey-cart drawn by a royal white Abyssinian donkey. In every sense her visit was too late. The tragedy was that she herself had blocked an earlier suggestion that the Prince and Princess of Wales should please the Irish by acquiring a home there. That would have done more good than her last minute descent. Her wish to be loved in Ireland, which her tour expressed, was touching and pathetic rather than effective.

Back in England the family news was bad. Her much loved second son Affie, Duke of Coburg, succumbed to throat cancer, his heir, Young Alfred, having already died of tuberculosis. What would happen to the beloved Duchy? The Queen's grandson, Christian Victor of Schleswig-Holstein, succumbed to enteric fever at Pretoria, a victim of the war; while at Kronberg the tragic Empress Frederick (Vicky) was dying of spine cancer.

The Queen's eyesight was worse than ever, though she could hardly be persuaded to wear 'hideous spectacles' in public. But again it was the war that roused her and, in her own words, she gave the Duke of Devonshire a piece of her mind for not keeping *The Times* 'straight' on the conflict. Her last public function was the Irish Industries Exhibition, which she insisted on attending. She left Windsor on 18 December for Osborne, never to see the castle again, as it turned out. The Widow of Windsor, that mainly euphonious, alliterative concept, was no more.

There was no sparkle in Christmas. Even Osborne's showy Durbar room had lost its brilliance. The Queen called 1900 a horrid year partly because the weather was so consistently dark. In reality the failure was in her eyes and general health. Her ladies could keep her awake during carriage drives only by constantly rearranging her cloaks and rugs. Then on Christmas morning they had to tell her that Jane, Lady Churchill, her oldest friend, had died of heart failure and the Queen trembled for poor Jane Churchill returning to the mainland in a gale.

For the last time, on 12 January 1901 she wrote up her journal, making the 13th the first blank day, apart from a few days after child-birth. She had first realised on 13 December 1861 that Albert might die. And so might the 13th prove fatal for her. Nevertheless she got through the 14th but sat throughout her usual carriage drive next day in a state of complete unawareness. Marie of Coburg, Affie's widow, sat beside her, hoping for a break in the clouds that did not come. On 16 January Sir James Reid took the doctor's responsibility of telling Ponsonby's office that she was ill.

On the 18th her children were sent for and on the 19th the first bulletin was issued. It was clearly hinted that the war in South Africa had been too much for her; and indeed the last soldier she saw was Lord Roberts KG, war hero, and the last minister Joseph Chamberlain, Colonial Secretary. She may even have guessed, while talking to Chamberlain, that her government was in collusion with the Jameson raiders of 1895–6. At any rate she knew what no one else did, that Chamberlain had paid a secret visit to Dr Jameson in prison, no doubt to make sure he kept his mouth shut.

After sinking and recovering for a day or two, Queen Victoria began her final decline, and those of her children who had temporarily left, returned to her bedside.

The end came peacefully on 22 January while her family were gathered round and Bishop Randall Davidson recited prayers and her favourite hymn, Newman's 'Lead kindly light'. By chance the Kaiser had been entertaining his cousin Arthur, Duke of Connaught, in Berlin when Arthur's summons came, so the Kaiser obeyed the summons too. He just wanted to see his Grandmama for the last time. Did he know that his Grandmama's last official act had been to tell the British Ambassador in Berlin to decline the Kaiser's offer of an honour? – respectfully, of course.

Though the Queen had always inveighed against crowded deathbed scenes with whole families assembled, saying she would never tolerate it in her own case, tradition was too strong for her. Her children had been calling out their own names round and round the bed, to hold her attention. At last they fell as silent as she. She died just after half-past six.

Queen Victoria's funeral was like another jubilee, being white and gold or purple, not black. She had insisted on that. No plumed or black horses, like the gloomy outfit she had once seen – once too often – at Balmoral. As head of the army she demanded a gun-carriage for the coffin, covered with a Union Jack. This she had. But the rope to drag the gun-carriage up the steep hill from the station into Windsor Castle broke, and the quick-thinking Ponsonby used the train's communication cord. Queen Victoria would have approved. She was a great communicator.

According to her wish there were no black draperies. How could her death be gloomy? Long ago she had recast her idea of the after-life: no eternal rest but an active and fulfilled existence, above all filled with Albert. She had first got her vision of a white, not black death from her poet laureate Alfred Tennyson. It is possible that her own deep black, worn from 1861 onwards and apparently in such contradiction to her settled ideas, belonged in her mind to a different category of mourning. The blackness of bereavement was indeed hers; the whiteness of death was Albert's – and now hers as well.

After a brief service in St George's Chapel, Windsor, she joined the Prince Consort in the luminous Frogmore Mausoleum. Her statue, also by the sculptor Marochetti, lay beside his. During the final service snow began to fall, joining the white snowdrops already flowering in the grass. The Queen had her white funeral.

EIGHT

QUEEN OF THE VICTORIAN AGE

There have been remarkable changes in the estimation of Queen Victoria's character this century. Her death was the signal for a revulsion against her and all she stood for. Everything Victorian was anathema. When the old Queen returned from Balmoral to Buckingham Palace for the last time the policeman on duty pointed to the Royal Standard floating from the roof and said: 'Mother's come 'ome.' Few girls born after 1901 were pleased to hear they had a Victorian mother. Victorian dress fashions and hair styles, furniture, family values, individual morals – all became regarded as boring, stuffy, prudish, dated.

Slowly the judgments and atmosphere changed again. Antique shops began to find Victoriana in growing demand. The change probably dates from Lytton Strachey's seminal biography of Queen Victoria, first published in 1921. As the ironical author of such 'eminent Victorian' pen-portraits as those of Cardinal Manning and Arnold of Rugby, he could be trusted not to pander to the Queen. Yet here he was presenting her as at once intriguing, touching, clever, original, alarming, impossible. If she could win over Strachey, as she clearly had, were there not other victories to her credit that even he had not noticed?

She was an amazing personality at a time when popular photography was only recently out of its infancy and when television and radio were not yet developed to spread the image and echo the voice. Her great physical charm was her voice, but hardly any of the public had heard it, apart from Eton boys lined up to honour her and such like; after one such occasion she said 'I thank you' in her clear, bell-like voice and they burst into cheering. True, the black Emperor of Abyssinia was sent a unique recording of the silver voice, but with instructions to destroy it after listening.

Of course she travelled about the country and the South of France a good deal and her physical appearance was well known. Queen Victoria was as high as possible on dignity and bearing, while her figure was comfortably middle-class: every inch a queen and every ounce a bourgeoise. The middle-class theme was developed by Lord Salisbury, her last Prime Minister, when he eulogised Queen Victoria after her death, as having been a kind of barometer of the people in their homes. He praised her interpretive powers: 'I have always felt that when I knew what the Queen thought I knew pretty certainly what view her subjects would take, and especially the middle class of her subjects . . .'

Lord Salisbury, for example, would have found the Queen and her subjects in favour of constitutional reform to the extent of giving the respectable working-class the vote – though no votes yet for any of the feminine sex. There were impressive moves on class by the Victorians, but only minimal moves on gender. Not that Queen Victoria stood for any such heresy as the classless society; indeed she expected her Court to set an example in class stability and mobility. There was a moment when the whole thing was openly challenged by no less a pillar of her life than her latest doctor, James Reid. A clever, delightful, middle-class Scot, Reid proposed marriage to one of the Queen's ladies, the Hon. Susan Baring, and was accepted. Horror of horrors! How could a Baring lower herself thus? But the final question for Her Majesty was not one of hypergamy but whether she could get on without Dr Reid. The answer was No, and the witty Reid broke the ice by promising never to do it again.

Other aspects of the Victorian Court, in addition to its class-consciousness, also invited criticism, particularly the Queen's life-style at Balmoral in later years – given the name of 'Balmorality'. It is through the younger of the royal children that intimate echoes of this situation are first heard. Prince Leopold was exceptionally spirited though a haemophiliac and in his lively letters to his sister Princess Louise, his punches at Balmoral's boredom were never pulled. For the public, however, all this was a closed book, and the Queen's Balmoral life undoubtedly enhanced the attractive, natural, healthy, popular impression made by her personality. Only one feature of Balmorality – if it could be called that – emerged to disturb the public. It was not the rationing of fires and ministers' cold bedrooms, but John Brown himself.

It seems unlikely that the alleged dalliance of Queen Victoria and Brown will be a proven discovery of the new millennium. The Deeside 'cache' of 'love letters', so far unpublished, does not seem likely to be of a new order of interest. Indeed it seems that the greetings cards in the 'cache' are much the same as Christmas and other cards already in the Royal Collection at Windsor. A Valentine from the Queen to Brown, quoted from the Deeside 'cache' appears to be identical with a card in the Archives: 'To my best friend JB from his best friend VRI.' It should be observed that the film, *Mrs Brown*, did not carry the message that the Queen and Brown were *lovers* in the full sense.

None of this means that their relationship was not most remarkable. For the Queen of England to say that her best friend was a gillie showed recklessness to say the least. Did she take account of possible Court jealousies? And what did she really mean by her best friend? After the Prince Consort's death she desperately felt the need of a strong man to look after her, as she said so often – Brown's 'strong arm'. When she got lamer and less mobile she missed Brown's strong arm more than ever she did in earlier days when passions were presumably running high. In one sense the person who really took the place of the deceased Brown was not a minister or even the Munshi but the 'Rubber'. Her masseuse kept her relatively active – and after her the wheel-chair . . .

Brown was mentioned in her will with gratitude, but along with her favourite dresser, as a very special servant. No one ever accused the Queen of living with the Munshi. In any case the Munshi was married and lived with his wife. Indeed there may sometimes have been an extra Indian wife, for the tongues that were shown to Sir James Reid during illness were often different. But they were never Queen Victoria's.

In an age that revelled in colonial empire it did Queen Victoria credit that she set an example in anti-racialism. As she said, England, with its worldwide ties, could not be racist; it was not the country for that sort of thing.

The Queen was probably relatively better with her far-flung colourful family than she was with her own. The most serious charges that can be brought against her as a mother are of interference, sometimes amounting to bullying; and the gravest differences she had with her two elder daughters were over breastfeeding their babies. It all began with Vicky, eldest of the five girls, deciding to nurse little Sigismund, her third son and fourth child. Queen Victoria was outraged and raised angry objections to Vicky's plan, some on grounds of delicacy but most on bogus grounds of health. The Queen was not mollified by the exquisite pleasure that Vicky touchingly said she got from nursing her child. Instead, the Queen wrote to Sir Charles Locock, her old doctor-friend of many years, suggesting he put the Queen's arguments against breastfeeding in a letter to the Princess Royal.[1] Victoria summed up Vicky's decision to nurse Siggie as being bad for mother and bad for baby. Her opening argument, written to Locock in the third person, ran as follows: 'Respecting this *foolish* nursing – the Queen wishes to ask Sir C. what *can* have made the Pcss. depart from sensible & natural rules adopted hitherto in her & in the *Queen's case* & do so without (as she ought to have done) consulting her Mother & Mother-in-law?' The above stated quite succinctly the Queen's matriarchal view.

The Queen went on to warn that the hot rooms and cold climate of Berlin would 'bring on abscesses & God knows what . . . and Vicky 'must *not* neglect her social duties & prefer being a *wet nurse*'. After expressing herself 'extremely annoyed & pained' by the Princess's 'impulsive nature & desire to have her own way', the Queen introduced her clinching arguments: the 'loss of that *one great & wise* adviser, her beloved father', who would have agreed. Other arguments that occurred here and elsewhere included the damage that nursing would do to Vicky's figure, whereas a good figure was needed for the proper performance of her social duties. And finally as a nervous and highly strung individual, Vicky was unsuited to the essentially animal duty of nursing. The more animal the wet nurse the better.

Queen Victoria found it hard to forgive her defiant daughter Vicky when she not only continued nursing her baby but persuaded her sister Alice to disgrace herself in the same way – by becoming a royal wet nurse. A few years later it looked as if a cruel fate had not forgiven Vicky either, for little Siggie turned out to be a haemophiliac. He died as a child.

These family differences, and of course others, were not disclosed until recently. Meanwhile, Queen Victoria was to enter history as a virtually perfect example of one who had a successful family life. There is the story of two ladies leaving the theatre after a performance of *Antony and Cleopatra*; says one to the other: 'How different, how *very* different from the home life of our own dear Queen!'

If she gave her children too little liberty, she was a supremely caring parent, and they knew it. Her last word was 'Bertie' – though some people said it was 'Albert' – and whatever her faults as a mother, she was seldom far away from children, six grandchildren and seven dogs romping around her on the lawn. Her great-grandchildren or friends' grandchildren were usually trailing after her to watch the spectacle of her being dressed. Little David of York (Edward VIII) would try to haul Gangan out of her chair and, having failed, call on Abdul the Munshi: 'Man pull it!'

With the modern world of human values she was more in touch than the Prince Consort had been; and not surprisingly, since he died almost forty years before her. It was he who forbade even the innocent parties in divorce to attend at Court; she who allowed them.

In the coming millennium Queen Victoria will certainly take her place in the hierarchy of great queens. How many queens have had their age named after them? Only one other: Queen Elizabeth I. In Victoria's case, long life and powerful personality did it. What today might commonly be called the 'toffee-nosed' side of her nature has long since been forgotten, to be replaced by a more accurate and complex view of her personality. The phrase that was once used to destroy her – 'We are not amused' – has since been destroyed. No one knows if or when she used it. Was it when a lady's dog lifted its leg in the Windsor grand corridor? Invention. But her journal is full of its opposite: 'I was very much amused.' If she laughed too boisterously when

Napoleon III upset his coffee in his cocked hat, that was the way of the Victorian world.

Not a few foreigners would have liked to have had her for their Queen too. Peasants in the South of France touched her for sanctity and luck. The fish-wives of Nice kissed her on both cheeks. Among the millions of mugs manufactured for her jubilees, some bore the inscription: '*The Centre of a World's Desire*'. That may have been making the same mistake as the map-makers of old. Still, she was a very great Queen.

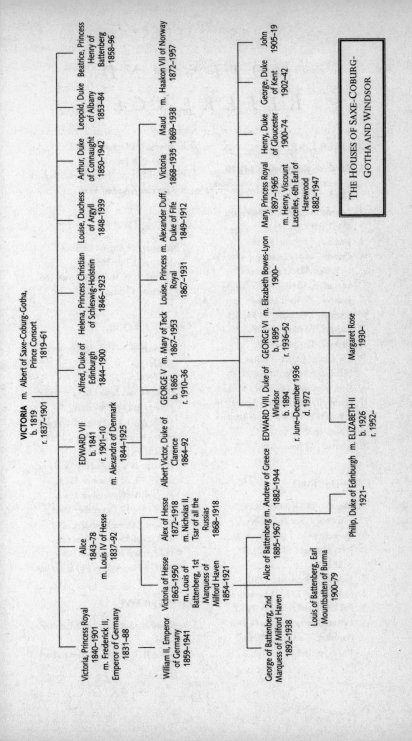

THE HOUSES OF SAXE-COBURG-GOTHA AND WINDSOR

NOTES AND REFERENCES

CHAPTER ONE

1. Elizabeth Longford, *Victoria RI*, (London, Weidenfeld & Nicolson, 1987), p. 28.
2. Lehzen to Queen, 2 December 1867, RA Y23/81.
3. Journal, 2 February 1838.
4. Prince Charles Leiningen's memo to Prince Albert's German Librarian, 1840, RA M7/67.
5. Journal, 29 April 1838.
6. Journal, 2 February 1839, RA.
7. Journal, 22 March 1839.
8. Journal, 17 April 1839.
9. *The Letters of Queen Victoria, a Selection from Her Majesty's Correspondence, 1837–61*, 3 vols (London, John Murray Ltd, 1908), I: I, p. 163. Queen to Melbourne, 9 May 1839.
10. Journal, 27 June 1839.

CHAPTER TWO

1. Journal, 11 October 1839; Viscount Esher *The Girlhood of Queen Victoria*, 2 vols (London, John Murray Ltd, 1912), II, p. 263.
2. Journal, 2 February 1840.
3. *Letters* I: i, p. 213, 31 January 1840.
4. RA Z491, 10 February 1840.
5. Lytton Strachey, *Queen Victoria*, (London, Chatto & Windus, 1922), p. 164.

6. Journal, 1 October 1842.
7. Journal, 8 June 1846.
8. *Letters* I: ii, p. 167, 4 April 1848.
9. Journal, 6 August 1848.

CHAPTER THREE

1. Journal, 22 August 1850.
2. Journal, 3 July 1850.
3. *Letters* I: ii, p. 362, 3 February 1852.
4. Journal, 3 January 1852.

CHAPTER FOUR

1. *Letters* I: iii, p. 253, 25 October 1857.
2. RA Y206.
3. *Dearest Child, Letters between Queen Victoria and the Princess Royal, 1858–1861*, ed. Roger Fulford (London, Evans Brothers, 1964), p. 115, 15 June 1858.
4. Ibid., p. 205, 10 August 1859.
5. RA Z140, 22 October 1861.
6. Journal, 10 November 1857.
7. RA Z142, 14 December 1861.
8. Strachey, *Queen Victoria*, p. 217.
9. RA Queen Victoria's Journal, 1872, based on extracts from 1861, 9 November–14 December

CHAPTER FIVE

1. Kronberg Letters, 23 December 1865.
2. *Letters* II: i, p. 296, Queen to Earl

Russell, 22 January 1866.

3. Journal, January 1864.

4. Quoted in G.M. Trevelyan, *The Life of John Bright* (London, 1913), p. 399.

5. Kronberg Letters, Queen to Vicky, 28 December 1867.

6. Philip Montefiore Magnus, *Gladstone: a Biography* (London, John Murray, 1954), p. 193.

7. Queen to Princess Royal, 21 April 1866, quoted in James Pope-Hennessy, *Queen Mary, 1867–1953* (London, G. Allen Unwin, 1959), p. 38.

8. Kronberg Letters, 4 January 1878.

9. *Letters* II: ii, p. 655.

10. Ibid., II: ii, p. 37–8.

11. Ibid., II: iii, p. 163.

12. Ibid., p. 166, 25 December 1880.

13. Kronberg Letters, 23 May 1881.

14. *Letters*, 9 March 1883.

15. RA VIC. ADD. MSS A12/899.

16. RA AA, 10 and 13.

17. Kronberg Letters, 29 March 1884.

18. *Letters* II: iii, p. 597.

19. Arthur Ponsonby, *Henry Ponsonby, Queen Victoria's Private Secretary* (London, Macmillanm 1942), p. 206.

CHAPTER SIX

1. Ponsonby Letters, 23 February 1870.

2. Kronberg Letters, Queen to Princess Royal, 2, 9, and 17 March 1870.

3. Queen to Lord Hatherley, 10 August 1871, quoted in Guedalla, *The Queen and Mr Gladstone*, 2 vols (London, Hodder & Stoughton, 1938), I, pp. 299–300.

4. RA S27/129, 26 June 1873.

5. W.F. Monypenny and G.E. Buckle, *The Life of Benjamin Disraeli, Earl of Beaconsfield*, 6 vols (London, John Murray, 1910–20), VI, p. 463.

6. Ibid., p. 462.

7. *Letters* II: p. 428, 26 November 1875.

CHAPTER SEVEN

1. Queen to Lord Salisbury, 20 May 1886, Salisbury Papers, Christ Church, Oxford.

2. Journal, 20 June 1887.

3. Queen to Lord Salisbury, 11 March 1898, Salisbury Papers.

4. Lady Gwendolen Cecil, *Life of Robert, Marquis of Salisbury*, 4 vols (London, Hodder & Stoughton), III, p. 191.

5. Journal, 23 September 1896.

6. Queen to Bigge, 30 January 1897, *Letters* III: iii, p. 370.

CHAPTER EIGHT

1. Queen to Sir Charles Locock, RA VIC ADD C30/5.

BIBLIOGRAPHY

PRIMARY SOURCES

Dearest Child, Letters between Queen Victoria and the Princess Royal, 1858–1861, ed. Roger Fulford, London, Evans Brothers, 1964.

Kronberg Letters, The Letters of Queen Victoria to her Eldest Daughter, Royal Archives, Victorian Additional Manuscripts, Windsor Castle.

The Letters of Queen Victoria, a Selection from her Majesty's Correspondence, 1837–61, 3 vols, London, John Murray Ltd, 1908.

The Letters of Queen Victoria, a Selection from her Majesty's Correspondence, 1886–1901, 3 vols, London, John Murray Ltd, 1930.

Ponsonby, Henry, The Letters of Sir Henry Ponsonby to his Wife, 1865–96 [unpublished, cited in Longford, 1987].

Royal Archives (RA), The Royal Archives, Windsor Castle.

Royal Archives Victorian Additional Manuscripts (RA VIC ADD MSS), The Royal Archives, Windsor Castle.

Salisbury Papers, Christ Church, Oxford.

Victoria, Queen, Journal, preserved in the Royal Archives, Windsor Castle.

——, *Leaves from the Journal of our Life in the Highlands from 1848–1861*, (abridged edition), London, Folio Society, 1973)

——, *More Leaves . . .*, London: Smith Elder, 1884

SECONDARY SOURCES

Bennett, Daphne, *King Without a Crown: Albert, Prince Consort of Great Britain, 1819–1861*, London, Heinemann, 1977.

Blake, Robert, *Disraeli*, London, Oxford University Press, 1969.

Cecil, Lady Gwendolen, *Life of Robert, Marquis of Salisbury*, 4 vols, London, Hodder & Stoughton, 1921–32.

Esher, Viscount, *The Girlhood of Queen Victoria*, 2 vols, London, John Murray Ltd, 1912.

Guedalla, *The Queen and Mr Gladstone*, 2 vols, London, Hodder & Stoughton, 1938.

Jenkins, Roy, *Gladstone*, London, Macmillan, 1996.

Longford, Elizabeth, *Victoria RI*, London, Weidenfeld & Nicolson, 1987.

—— (ed.), *Darling Loosy, Letters to Princess Louise 1856–1939*, London, Weidenfeld & Nicolson, 1991.

Magnus, Philip Montefiore, *Gladstone: a Biography*, London, John Murray, 1954.

Monypenny, W.F. and Buckle, G.E., *The Life of Benjamin Disraeli, Earl of Beaconsfield*, 6 vols, London, John Murray, 1910–20.

Ponsonby, Arthur, *Henry Ponsonby, Queen Victoria's Private Secretary*, London, Macmillan, 1942.

Pope-Hennessy, James, *Queen Mary, 1867–1953*, London, G Allen Unwin, 1959.

Strachey, Lytton, *Queen Victoria*, London, Chatto & Windus, 1922.

Weintraub, Stanley, *Victoria: Biography of a Queen*, London, John Murray, 1996.